PRAISE FOR

21st Century Skills: Learning for Life in Our Times

"Trilling and Fadel describe in very readable, practical terms how to infuse 21st century skills from standards all the way into the classroom. The DVD is full of wonderful 'ah-ha' moments to illustrate the possibilities. A terrific traveling companion for educators, parents, and business and government decision makers concerned about the future of our kids."

> —Paige Johnson, 2009 Chair of the Partnership for 21st Century Skills; Global K–12 Manager, Intel Corporation

"Bernie Trilling and Charles Fadel have written a book that is truly visionary, providing sound insight into education in the 21st century. Their book provides solid, practical advice for educators, policymakers, business leaders, and others interested in improving America's position in the global economy. I recommend it to anyone interested in maximizing classroom effectiveness in this digital age."

> —Dr. Steven L. Paine, West Virginia Superintendent of Schools

"A must-read for anyone interested in the ability of the United States to compete in a global economy. Educators, policymakers, business leaders, parents, and students will benefit from the comprehensive information on 21st century skills."

> —Mary Ann Wolf, executive director, State Educational Technology Directors Association (SETDA)

"Working, living, and learning in the 21st century will require an expanded set of skills, competencies, and flexibilities. We must prepare for a continuous learning and reskilling process throughout our lives and careers. This is a powerful exploration of what we collectively face as we live the future. A must-read!"

> —Elliott Masie, CEO and chair, The Learning Consortium

"Trilling and Fadel take the 21st century skills debate beyond rhetoric, providing a substantive, compelling, and engaging argument for the skills and competencies that our children need to succeed in a Knowledge Age economy. The skills they describe are the essential lifeblood of a productive, engaged, and intelligent citizenry—this book is a must-read for skeptics and enthusiasts alike!"

> —Margaret Honey, president and CEO, New York Hall of Science

"Hooray to Bernie Trilling and Charles Fadel for demystifying 21st century skills. This book makes clear why education must change: to help prepare students to meet complex challenges, fulfill their civic responsibilities, and live fulfilling lives. Full of crisp descriptions, *21st Century Skills* persuasively shows why policymakers and educators should run—not walk—to implement 21st century learning designs."

—John Wilson, executive director, National Education Association

"With *21st Century Skills,* Bernie Trilling and Charles Fadel have given us a global 'search and replace' for outdated educational thinking. Replace 'scope and sequence' with the '21st Century Learning Framework,' the P21 rainbow."

—Milton Chen, executive director, The George Lucas Educational Foundation

"Charles and Bernie's book cuts to the core challenge facing our country—is our education system preparing our children with the skills to succeed in a 'flat' 21st century world? Much more than a treatise on what is wrong with education, they provide a compelling vision for education as it should be and a road map for getting where we need to go."

—Keith R. Krueger, CEO, Consortium for School Networking (CoSN)

"This book presents an innovative, comprehensive strategy for evolving education to meet the needs of 21st century society."

—Chris Dede, Harvard School of Education

"The authors have done nothing less than provide a bold framework for designing a 21st century approach to education, an approach aimed at preparing all of our children to successfully meet the challenges of this brave, new world."

—Paul Reville, Secretary of Education, Commonwealth of Massachusetts

"It's about time that we have such an accessible and wise book about the 21st century skills that so many companies, policymakers, and educators are talking about."

—Roy Pea, Stanford University, professor of education and the learning sciences

"Trilling and Fadel lay out a comprehensive understanding of what is meant by 21st century skills. Read this book with a notepad—you'll be jotting down ideas for how to use the information in your school district. A must-read for superintendents, curriculum directors, and teachers."

—Anne L. Bryant, executive director, National School Boards Association

"*21st Century Skills* is full of interesting examples illustrating both what work will look like in the years ahead and how thoughtful educators are preparing children to thrive in tomorrow's workplaces. The richness of the examples reflects the authors' extensive knowledge of how work is changing in the nation's most innovative firms and their deep involvement in the efforts to improve America's schools."

—Richard J. Murnane, Thompson Professor of Education and Society, Harvard Graduate School of Education

"Trilling and Fadel have captured powerful insight into critical 21st century learning skills. Life goes on and so must learning—this book is a must for anyone interested in the future of education."

—Allan Weis, Former IBM vice president, founder of ThinkQuest and Advanced Network & Services

"*21st Century Skills* provides specific recommendations for how we can—indeed *must*—change the curriculum, teaching, assessment, use of technology, and the organization of our schools to better prepare students to be productive, creative citizens and workers in the global society and economy of the 21st century."

—Robert B. Kozma, Ph.D., emeritus director, Center for Technology in Learning, SRI International

"Bernie and Charles have presented a well-researched and futuristic framework for changing how we teach and learn for the 21st century. It will be up to all of us to accept this challenge and move our country and world into and beyond the 21st century."

—Kathy Hurley, senior vice president, Pearson K–12 Solutions and Pearson Foundation; Incoming Chair, The Partnership for 21st Century Skills

"This is a well-written and referenced road map for the complicated and interconnected collection of skills, knowledge, and attitudes that are essential for citizens to master in our increasingly complex and rapidly changing technological society."

—John E. Abele, Founding Chairman of the Board, Boston Scientific

"Inspirational and motivational, this book is a practical guide to implementing and understanding 21st century skills. Every teacher and parent should read it so they can prepare their children and their students to solve the problems of tomorrow, today."

—Dr. Barbara "Bobbi" Kurshan, executive director, Curriki

"After all the talk about organizing education, this book leads us back to what education is for. *21st Century Skills* is a comprehensive and elegant survey of our changing world, the skills it requires, and how those skills can be taught and learned. Here is a blueprint for 21st century schooling."

—Michael Stevenson, vice president, Global Education, Cisco

"This book presents an excellent case and road map for K–12 schools, for balancing content knowledge delivery with the development of necessary skills for success. It can serve as a valuable guide for parents, educators, and policymakers."

—Ioannis Miaoulis, Ph.D., president and director, Museum of Science, Boston

"For anyone who cares about the future of our children and their success in a global economy, *21st Century Skills* is required reading."

—Gerald Chertavian, chairman, Massachusetts Board of Elementary and Secondary Education's 21st Century Skills Task Force; founder and CEO, YearUp

"Bernie Trilling and Charles Fadel have been two of the essential intellects behind the growth of the 21st century skills movement. We have been asked for years to provide an in-depth treatment of the 21st century skills framework. Here it is."

—Ken Kay, executive director, Partnership for 21st Century Skills; CEO, e-Luminate Group

"Struggling to understand or explain the imperative for 21st century skills in our schools? Begin here."

—Julie A. Walker, executive director, American Association of School Librarians (AASL)

"*21st Century Skills: Learning for Life in Our Times* is a necessary and readable articulation of the reality of 21st century skills in educating today's generation of learners. Kudos to the authors for achieving clarity on this timely topic."

—Karen Cator, past chair, Partnership for 21st Century Skills

"Bernie Trilling and Charles Fadel have moved beyond the hype and buzz surrounding '21st century skills' to provide an insightful and commonsense guide to rethink learning and teaching in a world that urgently demands innovative, inventive, self-motivated and self-directed, creative problem solvers to confront increasingly complex global problems."

—Paul Reynolds, CEO, FableVision

21ST CENTURY SKILLS

|

LEARNING FOR LIFE
IN OUR TIMES

Bernie Trilling and Charles Fadel

JOSSEY-BASS
A Wiley Imprint
www.josseybass.com

Published by Jossey-Bass
A Wiley Imprint
One Montgomery Street, Suite 1200, San Francisco, CA 94104-4594—www.josseybass.com

Jossey-Bass books and products are available through most bookstores. To contact Jossey-Bass directly call our Customer Care Department within the U.S. at 800-956-7739, outside the U.S. at 317-572-3986, or fax 317-572-4002.

Wiley also publishes its books in a variety of electronic formats and by print-on-demand. Some material included with standard print versions of this book may not be included in e-books or in print-on-demand. If the version of this book that you purchased references media such as CD or DVD that was not included in your purchase, you may download this material at http://booksupport.wiley.com. For more information about Wiley products, visit www.wiley.com.

Library of Congress Cataloging-in-Publication Data

Trilling, Bernie.
21st century skills: learning for life in our times / Bernie Trilling and Charles Fadel.
p. cm.
Includes bibliographical references and index.
ISBN 978-0-470-47538-6 (cloth/dvd)
ISBN 978-1-118-15706-0 (paper/dvd)
1. Educational planning—United States. 2. Education—Aims and objectives—United States. 3. Educational change—United States. 4. Life skills—Study and teaching—United States. I. Fadel, Charles. II. Title.
LA217.2.T75 20009
370.73—dc22   2009021545

Printed in the United States of America
FIRST EDITION
HB Printing   10 9 8 7 6 5
PB Printing   10 9 8 7 6 5 4 3 2 1

CONTENTS

Figures and Tables   xi

Foreword to the Paperback Edition   xiii

The Authors   xxi

Prologue: The Search for Innovative Learning   xxv

Introduction: Learning to Innovate, Innovating Learning   xxix

     The Four Question Exercise   xxx

     About This Book   xxxiv

     A Map of the Book   xxxv

Part One: What Is 21st Century Learning?

1 Learning Past and Future   3

     Learning a Living: The Future of Work and Careers   7

     Learning Through Time   11

2 The Perfect Learning Storm: Four Converging Forces   21

     Knowledge Work   24

     Thinking Tools   25

     Digital Lifestyles   27

     Learning Research   30

     The Forces of Resistance   35

     The Turning of Learning: Toward a New Balance   36

     The Top 21st Century Challenge   40

Part Two: What Are 21st Century Skills?

3 Learning and Innovation Skills: Learning to Create Together   45

The Knowledge-and-Skills Rainbow   47

Learning to Learn and Innovate   49

Critical Thinking and Problem Solving   50

Communication and Collaboration   54

Creativity and Innovation   56

4 Digital Literacy Skills: Info-Savvy, Media-Fluent, Tech-Tuned   61

Information Literacy   65

Media Literacy   67

ICT Literacy   68

5 Career and Life Skills: Work-Ready, Prepared for Life   73

Flexibility and Adaptability   75

Initiative and Self-Direction   77

Social and Cross-Cultural Interaction   80

Productivity and Accountability   82

Leadership and Responsibility   84

Part Three: 21st Century Learning in Practice

6 21st Century Learning and Teaching   89

Learning P's and Q's: Problems and Questions   90

Roads to Answers and Solutions: Science and Engineering   91

7 Powerful Learning: Proven Practices, Researched Results   95

The 21st Century Project Learning Bicycle   96

Creativity Through Projects 104

Evidence That Project Learning Works 107

Obstacles to Collaborative Inquiry and Design Learning 114

8 Retooling Schooling: Reshaping Support Systems 117

Shifting Systems in Sync 120

Support Systems 125

From Skills to Expertise: Future Learning
Frameworks 145

**9 Conclusion: Learning for Life—Building a
Better World 151**

Appendix A Resources 159

21st Century Skills Example Videos DVD 159

Resources from the Partnership for
21st Century Skills 161

Selected Online Resources 162

**Appendix B About the Partnership for 21st Century
Skills 167**

What Is P21? 167

What Does P21 Do? 168

How the P21 Learning Framework Came into Being 170

Appendix C 3Rs × 7Cs = 21st Century Learning 175

Acknowledgments 179

Notes 183

References 187

Credits 197

How to Use the DVD 199

Index 201

FIGURES AND TABLES

Figures

1.1.	Value Chains Then and Now	4
1.2.	Signs for Our Times	6
1.3.	New Skills for 21st Century Work	8
1.4.	The Future of 21st Century Work	10
2.1.	21st Century Learning Convergence	23
2.2.	21st Century Learning Balance	38
3.1.	SARS Web Site Screenshot	47
3.2.	The 21st Century Knowledge-and-Skills Rainbow	48
3.3.	Creative Whack Pack Creativity Cards	60
4.1.	The 21st Century Knowledge-and-Skills Rainbow	65
5.1.	The 21st Century Knowledge-and-Skills Rainbow	75
6.1.	Science and Technology, Questions and Problems	92
7.1.	Student and Teacher Project Wheels	99
7.2.	The Project Learning Bicycle	100
7.3.	The 21st Century Project Learning Bicycle Model	102
8.1.	Systems Diagram of School Interactions	118
8.2.	21st Century Learning Framework	119
8.3.	West Virginia Grade 11 Social Studies Test Question	133
8.4.	New Learning Environments	140
8.5.	Knowledge Age Value Chain	146
8.6.	Possible Future 21st Century Learning Framework	149
9.1.	The "Big E" Global Problems	157
B.1.	21st Century Learning Framework	173
C.1.	21st Century Learning Outcomes	175

Tables

1.1.	Jobs and 21st Century Work	9
1.2.	Society's Educational Goals Throughout the Ages	14
5.1.	Performance Evaluation Criteria	74
6.1.	Scientific Versus Engineering Methods	93
8.1.	Grade 5 Science Standard from West Virginia	127
C.1.	P21 and 7C Skills	176

FOREWORD

TO THE PAPERBACK EDITION

Every big project seems to have its share of unexpected twists and turns, gathering a life of its own as it progresses. The paperback you now hold is just one of the many excursions this book project has taken us on. To our delight, expanding interest in the perspectives and guidance offered here has prompted not only a more widely available paperback edition and an enhanced e-book version, but also translations into Mandarin and other languages.

Since this book's first release, we've had the extraordinary privilege of meeting, speaking, and connecting with thousands of readers like you, all striving to do what they can to better prepare our students for learning and life in the 21st century. We are continually amazed at the passion, dedication, energy, and innovation that educators, parents, and leaders everywhere are bringing to the challenge of helping students and schools be more successful in very challenging times.

We now know just how powerful and widespread the global 21st century learning movement has become. Just two examples of the many positive developments are:

- The Organisation for Economic Co-operation and
  Development (OECD)—the developers of the widely
  adopted PISA international student evaluations—and its

thirty-four member countries have announced a large-scale Skills Strategy initiative to investigate issues such as the value of occupation-specific versus basic and generic skills, the extent and impact of a mismatch between available skills and those needed in the labor market, and the best practices of member countries in providing the education and training needed to build essential 21st century skills (http://www .oecd.org/document/6/0,3746,en_2649_33723_47414086_ 1_1_1_1,00.html).

- Forty-four U.S. states have adopted a new set of education standards that includes some of the key 21st century skills outlined in this book, and the Partnership for 21st Century Skills (P21) has released a toolkit to help educators better integrate these skills into education practice (http://www .p21.org/index.php?option=com_content&task=view&id= 1005&Itemid=236).

The global 21st century learning conversation has graduated beyond the "either/or" debate around knowledge and skills and is now firmly focused on how to best develop the "both/and" range of knowledge, skills, dispositions, and expertise most needed for our times. Recent developments in neuroscience have also confirmed that knowledge can best be learned through its real-world applications, and that an internal "need to know" can provide the motivation necessary for learning complex and challenging content.

We have both experienced firsthand the new sense of urgency for education change as the aftershocks of the Great Recession continue to take their toll on economies, communities, and lives everywhere:

- Unemployment is hovering at painfully high levels in communities all over the world, with youth unemployment reaching critically high levels.
- Wrenching shifts in the global patterns of work—due to increasing automation, use of communication and transportation technologies, and job migration—are having deeper impacts on employment and economic opportunity.
- Funding for education and other social services is under great stress.
- The global specter of rising energy and food costs is further straining budgets.
- The impacts of natural disasters due to extreme weather and climate change are adding further challenges.

We are hearing with increasing frequency a key question asked with growing concern:

> How can we help our students learn what is necessary to be prepared for the jobs that might be there when they graduate, and for the kinds of problems they will face in a more uncertain, rapidly shifting, competitive and connected world?

The questions covered in this book—education for what, why, and how—are not theoretical. They are real and urgent issues.

We have all seen in the so-called Arab Spring countries and beyond the kinds of unrest that can arise when large numbers of under-thirty, tech-connected, traditionally educated, urban youth are confronted with a severe lack of jobs and a strong desire for a better life, yet little hope of achieving it. Education, the economy, jobs, politics, and social harmony are intimately linked.

We have also seen firsthand that with planning and persistence, solid progress toward a 21st century education can be achieved. The experiences of countries like Australia, Finland, South Korea, Scotland, and Singapore have shown us that transforming education systems is very hard work, demanding consistent, long-term commitments to changing learning approaches—a consistency that must survive shifts in politics and administrations. The benefits of having students better prepared for college, career, and civic life are more than worth it—they are absolutely necessary for the future health and welfare of every citizen, economy, and society.

The good news is that despite immense challenges, more schools, school districts, school networks, states and provinces, and even entire education systems and countries are moving closer to the principles and practices set out in these pages. Some of the pioneering 21st century schools highlighted in the videos included with this book are now connecting with other like-minded school networks to share and improve their learning approaches and expand their impacts. A shining example is a collective of eight school networks with over four hundred elementary and secondary schools in over forty U.S. states and a number of other countries, supported in part by the William and Flora Hewlett Foundation's Deeper Learning initiative (http://www.hewlett.org/programs/education-program/deeper-learning).

An essential question one of us was asked to research for this initiative was, "What principles and practices do these pioneering, deeper learning school networks have in common?" A simple first step toward finding the answer was to create a "Wordle" (visual diagram of the most common words used) of the core principles each network values. The result was revealing:

The diagram gives you a sense of the importance of student-centeredness in learning, the value of authentic projects, student interests, relationships and pathways to success, and the globally connected nature of their learning.

Through hours of interviews, observations, and discussions with school leaders, teachers, and students from these networks of schools, a pattern of common practices emerged. They include:

1. *Learning*—deeply engaging, personalized, and collaborative learning motivated by relevant questions and deep inquiry, problems and the design of creative solutions, and real-world issues and challenging projects, all with a focus on high-quality student work

2. *Teaching*—teachers as learning designers, model learners, mentors, guides, and school leaders

3. *Evaluation*—student work evaluated through public presentations and by a variety of authentic performance assessments incorporated into everyday learning

4. *Culture/Climate*—for both students and educators, a professional culture of high expectations, responsibility, ownership, and self-direction; and a personal culture of caring, respect, trust, cooperation, and community

5. *Development*—teacher and student development focused on improving the quality of student work through collaboration and embedded coaching, modeling, mentoring, and leadership

6. *Tools*—pervasive use of technology and other learning resources to support Deeper Learning outcomes and practices

These practices may be the vital components of an emerging common "ecosystem" of learning for the 21st century. Stay tuned.

We look forward to hearing about your own journeys and projects on the road to 21st century learning—please share these with us on the book's Web site:

http://www.21stcenturyskillsbook.com/contact.php

We welcome opportunities to assist you in helping all your students acquire the 21st century skills and expertise needed for a successful work life, a happy family life, an active community life, and a lifetime of enjoyable learning.

Bernie Trilling
Charles Fadel
January 2012

To the 22nd century learners who will surely wonder what all the fuss was about and why it was so hard for everyone in the 21st century to do the obvious!
—Bernie and Charles

To Jennifer, Samara, Jeremy, Oriana, and my extended family and friends who keep my learning real, honest, relevant, deep, and everlasting.

And to the parents and teachers of the world's children who shape our future each day.

May that future be bright, caring, green, and full of hope.
—Bernie

To my daughter, Nathalie, with all my forever-unconditional love.

To my mother, Aline, for teaching me open-mindedness through example.

To Ray Stata, founder of Analog Devices Inc., who in 1990 kindled my passion for education through his presentation "Accelerating the Rate of Learning."

And to the little girl in Santo Domingo, whose eyes will forever remind me that "a mind is a terrible thing to waste."

May you, and the many millions like you, find the dignity, happiness, and serenity you deserve, through the transformational power of education.
—Charles

THE AUTHORS

The co-authors of this book, Bernie Trilling and Charles Fadel, have long been completing each other's sentences in their work to bring education into the 21st century. As past co-chairs of the Standards, Assessment and Professional Development Committee of the Partnership for 21st Century Skills (P21), they helped craft the breakthrough "rainbow" learning framework which has become an international symbol for the 21st century learning movement.

Though they both have been deeply involved in the development of innovative technologies to reshape learning, Bernie and Charles share a deep conviction that the most important learning tools are our minds, our hearts, and our hands, all working together.

Bernie Trilling is the founder and CEO of 21st Century Learning Advisors and a recognized thought leader, advisor, consultant, author, and keynote speaker. As the former global director of the Oracle Education Foundation, he directed the development of education strategies, partnerships, and services for the Foundation and its ThinkQuest programs. He has served as board member of the Partnership for 21st Century Skills and co-chaired the committee that developed the P21 "rainbow" learning framework.

Bernie has worked on a number of pioneering educational products and services and is an active member of a variety of organizations dedicated to bringing 21st century learning methods to students and teachers across the globe.

Prior to joining the Oracle Education Foundation, Bernie was Director of the Technology in Education group at WestEd, a U.S. national educational laboratory, where he led a team of educational technologists in integrating technology into both the instructional and administrative realms of education. He has also served in a variety of roles in both education and industry, including executive producer for instruction at Hewlett-Packard Company, where he helped lead a pioneering, state-of-the-art global interactive distance learning network.

As an instructional designer and educator, Bernie has held a number of professional educational roles in settings ranging from preschool to corporate training. He has written dozens of articles for educational journals and magazines, is a frequent keynote speaker at educational conferences, and has been a featured guest on a wide variety of national and international media.

Bernie attended Stanford University where he studied environmental science and education. Applying his studies to the real world, he helped organize the first Earth Day in Washington, D.C.

Recently, Bernie has been researching the common practices of over 400 schools that are models for 21st century learning as part of the Hewlett Foundation's Deeper Learning initiative.

Bernie is a lifelong, self-propelled learner. He has devoted much of his career to furthering the kinds of learning experiences he has found most engaging, collaborative, relevant, and powerful, working to make these experiences available to learners of all ages.

Charles Fadel is a global education thought leader and expert, author, and inventor with several affiliations:

- Visiting practitioner at Harvard's Graduate School of Education; visiting lecturer at Wharton/UPenn's CLO program; member of the President's Council at Olin College; senior fellow, Human Capital at The Conference Board
- Vice-chair of the Education Committee of the Business and Industry Advisory Committee to the Organisation for Economic Co-operation and Development (OECD)
- Formerly Global Education Lead at Cisco Systems, and its liaison with UNESCO and the World Bank
- Board member at Innovate/Educate. Former board member at the Partnership for 21st Century Skills, and Change the Equation
- Angel investor with Beacon Angels (http://beaconangels. wordpress.com/members/)

He has worked on education projects with more than thirty countries and states, both developed and developing. His work spans schools, higher education, and workforce development. He has been featured by National Public Radio, the CBC, Huffington Post, and many other media.

Charles has been awarded five patents and worked in the ICT industry (semiconductors and systems) for more than twenty years in his career. He holds a bachelor of science degree in electronics/physics with a minor in neuroscience, and a master of business administration in international marketing.

| PROLOGUE |

THE SEARCH FOR INNOVATIVE LEARNING

O
ur visitors were a distinguished delegation of education officials from the Chinese Ministry of Education. They had come to see with their own eyes the U.S. schools they had heard were innovating in teaching and learning.

At the Napa New Tech High School in Northern California, a school famous for its project approach to learning, we were visiting a classroom that looked like a hybrid between a corporate conference room and a miniature media production studio. We were talking, with the help of an interpreter, to a group of students and their teacher, all very proud to show off their recent project work.

As part of their project, the students had recently implemented some clever conservation methods that were saving the school hundreds of dollars each month in utility costs. They also helped protect a nearby watershed from erosion by planting carefully chosen native shrubs and trees.

One of the Chinese delegates, Mr. Zheng, appeared increasingly excited the more he saw and heard. By the time we gathered to recap the day's experiences, he just couldn't wait to speak any longer.

He held up the school's curriculum guide and asked, in English, "Where in here do you teach creativity and innovation? I want to know how you teach this! We need our students to learn how to do this!"

The school's curriculum director, Paul, took a deep breath, collected his thoughts, smiled, and answered slowly, "I have some not-so-good news . . . and some good news.

"The not-so-good news is . . . it isn't in the curriculum guide.

"It's more in the air we breathe—or maybe the water we drink; the history of our country—Thomas Edison, Henry Ford, Benjamin Franklin; it's in our business culture, our entrepreneurs, our willingness to try new ideas; the tinkering and inventing in our garages, the challenge of tackling tough problems and the excitement of creating something new; in being rewarded for our new ideas, taking risks, failing, and trying again.

"In a strange way, our U.S. schools have been becoming more like your schools in China, focused on learning what will be tested in the big exams that determine so much of a student's future. Our school is trying to keep the spirit of innovation and invention alive in the projects we do. We believe these skills are essential to being successful in our new global economy and in helping to solve the problems we all face together."

Mr. Zheng, thinking deeply about all that it would take for today's Chinese traditional school culture to embrace a more innovative approach to learning, asked hopefully, "And what is the good news?"

Paul chuckled.

"Well, the good news is that with the right opportunity and support, we have seen that our students can learn to be more creative and innovative. But it takes good teachers to create the right balance—between learning the facts and principles, and coming up with new solutions to problems and creative answers to questions they really care about."

Mr. Zheng responded diplomatically, "Maybe we will help you better learn the principles and you will show us how to use them to be creative—we can work together."

We all laughed politely, shook hands, took the mandatory group photo in front of the school, and our distinguished visitors were off to their next stop.

INTRODUCTION

LEARNING TO INNOVATE, INNOVATING LEARNING

This is a book about hopeful change coming to education and learning. It's also about rekindling the love of learning inside us all and the joy of working together to help create a better world—something we all could use right now.

Wherever we go in our education travels these days, we seem to be carrying on one long global conversation with variations on the same themes and questions:

- How has the world changed, and what does this mean for education?
- What does everyone need to learn now to be successful?
- How should we learn all this?
- How is 21st century learning different from learning in the 20th century and what does it really look like?
- How will 21st century learning evolve through the century?
- How will a 21st century learning approach help solve our global problems?

The premise of this book is that the world has changed so fundamentally in the last few decades that the roles of learning and education in day-to-day living have also changed forever.

Though many of the skills needed in centuries past, such as critical thinking and problem solving, are even more relevant today, how these skills are *learned* and *practiced* in everyday life in the 21st century is rapidly shifting. And there are some new skills to master, such as digital media literacy, that weren't even imagined fifty years ago.

To help you get a better feel for the changes coming to education and learning, take a few minutes to join in on an informal thought experiment that many other educators, school leaders, and parents have been participating in. It's an exercise that makes the issue of learning for our times very personal and very real.

The Four Question Exercise

First, imagine (if it's not already the case) that you have a child, grandchild, a niece or nephew, or a child of friends whom you love and care about deeply, and this child is just starting preschool or kindergarten this year. Then consider the following questions, making notes as you go.

Question #1: *What will the world be like twenty or so years from now when your child has left school and is out in the world?* Think about what life was like twenty years ago and all the changes you have seen happen. Then imagine what will happen in the next twenty years.

Question #2: *What skills will your child need to be successful in this world you have imagined twenty years from now?*

Question #3: Now think about your own life and the times when you were really learning, so much and so deeply, that you would call these the "peak learning experiences" of your life. *What were the conditions that made your high-performance learning experiences so powerful?*

Before going on to Question #4, look over your answers to the first three questions and think about how most students currently spend their time each day in school. Then consider the final question:

Question #4: *What would learning be like if it were designed around your answers to the first three questions?*

We've done this exercise at the beginning of presentations with scores of diverse groups. The big surprise is that the answers to the four questions are amazingly consistent. No matter what their backgrounds are or where in the world they may be, audiences always end up with the same conclusion: it's high time that learning becomes *more in tune with the demands of our times and the needs of today's students.*

Question #1—*What will the world be like twenty years from now?*—evokes responses that project current events, issues, and challenges into the future. Samples of typical responses:

- A "smaller world," more connected by technology and transport
- A mounting information and media tidal wave that needs taming
- Global economic swings that affect everyone's jobs and incomes
- Strains on basic resources—water, food, and energy
- The acute need for global cooperation on environmental challenges
- Increasing concerns about privacy, security, and terrorism
- The economic necessity to innovate to be globally competitive

- More work in diverse teams spanning languages, cultures, geographies, and time zones
- The need for better ways to manage time, people, resources, and projects

Question #2—*What skills will your child need in the future you painted?*—inevitably generates most of the 21st century skills covered in this book, including values and behaviors such as curiosity, caring, confidence, and courage that often accompany the learning of these skills. The 21st century skills we cover in this book can be placed in three useful categories:

- Learning and innovation skills:
  Critical thinking and problem solving
  Communications and collaboration
  Creativity and innovation

- Digital literacy skills:
  Information literacy
  Media literacy
  Information and communication technologies (ICT)
      literacy

- Career and life skills:
  Flexibility and adaptability
  Initiative and self-direction
  Social and cross-cultural interaction
  Productivity and accountability
  Leadership and responsibility

Question #3—*What were the conditions that made your high-performance learning experiences so powerful?*—generates collective answers that are even more intriguing. The stories we've heard over the years often bring out these themes:

- Very high levels of learning challenge, often coming from an internal personal passion
- Equally high levels of external caring and personal support—a demanding but loving teacher, a tough but caring coach, or an inspirational learning guide
- Full permission to fail—safely, and with encouragement to apply the hard lessons learned from failure to continuing the struggle with the challenge at hand

This last point is extremely important. Failures, well supported, can often be better teachers than easy successes (though this is certainly not a very popular approach in today's "test success"–driven schools).

Question #4—*What would school be like if it were designed around your answers to Questions #1 through #3?*—consistently spotlights the distance between what we all know learning should be and what most schools end up doing each day:

- The world of work is increasingly made of teams working together to solve problems and create something new— why do students mostly work alone and compete with others for teacher approval?
- Technology is more a part of our children's lives each day— why should they have to check their technology at the classroom door and compete for limited school computer time?

- The world is full of engaging, real-world challenges, problems, and questions—why spend so much time on disconnected questions at the end of a textbook chapter?
- Doing projects on something one cares about comes naturally to all learners—why are learning projects so scarce inside so many classrooms?
- Innovation and creativity are so important to the future success of our economy—why do schools spend so little time on developing creativity and innovation skills?

As a whole, the Four Question exercise is a quick way for a group to collectively sketch a blueprint of the future of learning. Now, if only we could wave a magic wand and instantly realize the consensus results of these Four Question exercises, schools would be far different places!

About This Book

The good news is that schools all around the world are moving closer to learning designs we know our students need for 21st century success. Schools from Singapore to Sydney, Helsinki to Hong Kong, and the United Kingdom to the United States are innovating learning as their students learn how to innovate. A vibrant global movement is in play to retune the instruments of education for a rising band of digital learners, and to sync up learning to the new rhythms of the 21st century.

This book is about why and how the global landscape for learning is reshaping itself, and about what this global transformation, often called the 21st century skills movement, may bring to a school near you.

Parents, teachers, school administrators, and policymakers re-- quire a clear vision of what our children now need to learn to be successful. Everyone who cares about education and our future needs a new road map to help guide our explorations and journeys to an approach to learning geared for our times.

We hope this book will be a handy guidebook and a comforting traveling companion on the road to learning in the 21st century.

A Map of the Book

In Part One, Chapter One begins with a look at the rather bumpy beginning the 21st century has brought us, and the new roles education and learning are now playing. We take a look back at the historical role education has played on society's evolving stage, and then explore the world of work students will be graduating into and the prospects for future jobs and careers in the 21st century. Chapter Two examines the extraordinary forces converging on education, shifting learning to a new balance and altering both what we need to learn and how we will learn to be successful students, workers, and citizens of the 21st century. It also assesses the forces resisting change, and presents examples of the kinds of new learning most in tune with our times.

Part Two explains the nature of each of the key 21st century skills. Chapter Three introduces the framework that the Partnership for 21st Century Skills (P21) has developed to guide the evolution of the education landscape, then covers the first area of 21st century skills, learning to learn and innovate. The next two chapters describe the other two main areas, digital literacy in Chapter Four and career and life skills in Chapter Five. Each chapter gives examples of how these skills are being learned in an innovative learning project called ThinkQuest.

Part Three turns to the practical side of 21st century learning. Chapter Six looks at the two most powerful motivations for learning that we know of (but often forget in our rush to "cover" content): engaging questions and problems. Chapter Seven then introduces a new framework for 21st century learning practice driven by questions and problems—the 21st century project learning "Bicycle model." The role design might play in meeting the rising demand for creativity and innovation in the emerging Innovation Age is also investigated.

Chapter Eight discusses the research and evidence base that validates the learning value of this model and its powerful learning methods. That chapter also explores how each of the educational support systems of the P21 framework are working together to move learning toward a 21st century design. It concludes with a glimpse of a possible future learning framework—how our current models for 21st century learning will evolve from skills-based to expertise-based.

Chapter Nine, the Conclusion, offers a vision of how future societies may place learning more at the heart of culture and what a future learning network of schools and online services might mean for the global citizens of tomorrow. It closes with a focus on the urgent global challenges of our times and how learning can engage students and citizens around the world in collaborative 21st century design projects that contribute to creating a better world and to more meaningful and memorable learning.

Three Appendixes offer a useful list of 21st century learning resources, a brief history of the Partnership for 21st Century Skills and its learning framework, and a handy formula for remembering the key 21st century skills.

The crux of success or failure is to know which core values to hold on to, and which to discard and replace when times change.

—Jared Diamond

The illiterate of the 21st Century are not those that cannot read or write, but those that cannot learn, unlearn, and relearn.

—Alvin Toffler

I'm calling on our nation's governors and state education chiefs to develop standards and assessments that don't simply measure whether students can fill in a bubble on a test, but whether they possess 21st century skills like problem-solving and critical thinking and entrepreneurship and creativity.

—President Barack Obama

| PART ONE |

WHAT IS 21ST CENTURY LEARNING?

1

Learning Past and Future

We are currently preparing students for jobs that don't yet
exist ... using technologies that haven't yet been invented ...
in order to solve problems we don't even know are problems yet.
—Richard Riley, Secretary of Education under Clinton

It happened quietly, without fanfare or fireworks.

In 1991, the total money spent on Industrial Age goods in
the United States—things like engines and machines for agriculture, mining, construction, manufacturing, transportation,
energy production, and so on—was exceeded for the first time
in history by the amount spent on information and communications technologies: computers, servers, printers, software, phones,
networking devices and systems, and the like.

The score? In 1991, "Knowledge Age" expenditures exceeded
Industrial Age spending by $5 billion ($112 billion versus $107
billion). That year marked year one of a new age of information,
knowledge, and innovation.[1] Since then, countries around the
globe have increasingly been spending more on making, manipulating, managing, and moving bits and bytes of information than
on handling the material world's atoms and molecules.

This monumental shift from Industrial Age production to
that of the Knowledge Age economy—information-driven, globally networked—is as world-changing and life-altering as the shift
from the Agrarian to the Industrial Age three hundred and fifty
years ago.

Moving from a primarily nuts-and-bolts factory and manufacturing economy to one based on data, information, knowledge, and expertise has had a huge impact on the world's economies and our everyday lives. The sequence of steps to produce a product or service, the so-called value chain of work, has dramatically shifted, as shown in Figure 1.1.

Industrial economies are focused on turning natural resources such as iron and crude oil into products we use—automobiles and gasoline. Knowledge economies turn information, expertise, and technological innovations into services we need, like medical care and cell phone coverage.

This of course doesn't mean that Industrial Age work will or can go away in the Knowledge Age—manufactured products will always be needed.

It does mean that with increasing automation and the shifting of manufacturing (and its environmental impacts) to lower-wage, industrial-equipped countries such as China, India, and Brazil, industrial work in Knowledge Age countries will continue

Industrial Age Value Chain

Extraction ⟶ Manufacturing ⟶ Assembly ⟶ Marketing ⟶ Distribution ⟶ Products (and Services)

Knowledge Age Value Chain

Data ⟶ Information ⟶ Knowledge ⟶ Expertise ⟶ Marketing ⟶ Services (and Products)

Figure 1.1. Value Chains Then and Now.

to decline and service-based *knowledge work* will continue to grow well into the 21st century.

But that's only one of a whole bundle of big changes that have arrived at our doorstep in the early part of the 21st century. And these changes will continue to make new demands on education as the century progresses.

As Thomas Friedman vividly reported in *The World Is Flat: A Brief History of the Twenty-First Century* and in *Hot, Flat, and Crowded*, the 21st century is challenging and reshuffling the very foundations of our society in new, powerful, and often alarming ways. For example:

- The world now has a truly global financial and economic ecosystem. This highly interlinked system means that a disruption in one part of the world (such as a U.S. housing loan crisis) has dire consequences to economies everywhere.
- The growing disparity in the world between rich and poor leads to social tension, conflicts, extremism, and a less safe world for everyone.

Yet the biggest challenge to the survival of all societies is the strain we're placing on our physical environment:

- Global population has risen from 2.5 billion in 1950 to nearly 7 billion in 2009. This figure is expected to exceed 9 billion by 2050.
- Despite widespread poverty, increasing numbers of people are rising into middle-class lifestyles, which drastically increases their consumption of the earth's material and energy resources.

- Increased consumption of resources is causing climate change and other threats to the natural world and its global life-support systems.

Add up overpopulation, overconsumption, increased global competition and interdependence, melting ice caps, financial meltdowns, and wars and other threats to security, and you get quite a bumpy beginning for our new century!

But as the Chinese characters for the word *crisis* (shown in Figure 1.2) suggest, in times such as these, along with danger and despair come great opportunities for change and renewed hope.

One of education's chief roles is to prepare future workers and citizens to deal with the challenges of their times. Knowledge work—the kind of work that most people will need in the coming decades—can be done anywhere by anyone who has the expertise, a cell phone, a laptop, and an Internet connection. But to have expert knowledge workers, every country needs an education system that produces them; therefore, *education becomes the key to economic survival in the 21st century.*

To further understand what our times demand of education we must take a closer look at the changing world of 21st century work.

$$危机$$

wei   *ji*

(danger) (opportunity)

Figure 1.2. Signs for Our Times.

Learning a Living:
The Future of Work and Careers

A few years ago, four hundred hiring executives of major corporations were asked a very simple but significant question: "Are students graduating from school really ready to work?" The executives' collective answer? Not really.[2]

The study clearly showed that students graduating from secondary schools, technical colleges, and universities are sorely lacking in some basic skills and a large number of applied skills:

- Oral and written communications
- Critical thinking and problem solving
- Professionalism and work ethic
- Teamwork and collaboration
- Working in diverse teams
- Applying technology
- Leadership and project management

Reports from around the world confirm that this "21st century skills gap" is costing business a great deal of money. Some estimate that well over $200 billion a year is spent worldwide in finding and hiring scarce, highly skilled talent, and in bringing new employees up to required skill levels through costly training programs. And as budgets tighten further in tough economic times, companies need highly competent employees ready to hit the ground running without extra training and development costs.

The competitiveness and wealth of corporations and countries is completely dependent on having a well-educated workforce—as one 2006 report called it, "Learning Is Earning." Improving a country's literacy rate by a small amount can have huge positive economic impacts. Education also increases the earning potential of workers—an additional year of schooling can improve a person's lifetime wages by 10 percent or more.[3]

So why is education falling short in preparing students for 21st century work?

The world of Knowledge Age work requires a new mix of skills. Jobs that require routine manual and thinking skills are giving way to jobs that involve higher levels of knowledge and applied skills like expert thinking and complex communicating (see Figure 1.3).

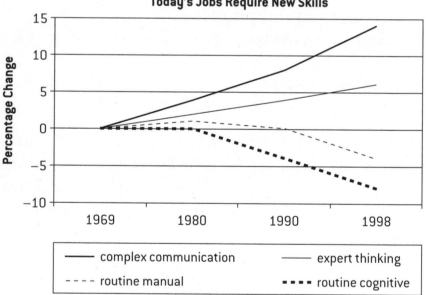

Figure 1.3.   New Skills for 21st Century Work.

Source: Adapted from Levy and Murnane, 2004.

Table 1.1 lists examples of jobs requiring routine and manual skills and those with high demands for complex communicating and thinking skills.

The rising demand for a highly skilled workforce also means that there will be a growing income gap between less educated, relatively unskilled workers and highly educated, highly skilled workers. Routine tasks are increasingly being automated, and the routine jobs still done by people barely pay a living wage. Routine work is moving to countries where the cost of labor is very low, as shown in Figure 1.4.

Our world's education systems must now prepare as many students as possible for jobs at the top of the chart—the high-paying

Table 1.1.   Jobs and 21st Century Work.

Type of Task	Task Description	Example Occupations
Routine	Rules-based Repetitive Procedural	Bookkeepers Assembly line workers
Manual	Environmental adaptability Interpersonal adaptability	Truck drivers Security guards Waiters Maids and janitors
Complex thinking and communicating	Abstract problem solving Mental flexibility	Scientists Attorneys Managers Doctors Designers Software programmers

Source: Adapted from Autor, 2007.

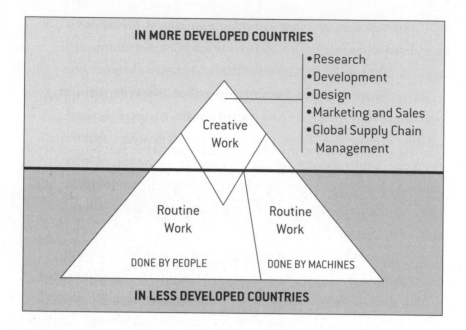

Figure 1.4. The Future of 21st Century Work.

Source: Adapted from National Center on Education and the Economy, 2007.

knowledge work jobs of today and tomorrow that require complex skills, expertise, and creativity. And many of the jobs of the future do not even exist today!

If all these changes weren't quite enough, students in school today can expect to have more than eleven different jobs between the ages of eighteen and forty-two.[4] We don't know yet how many more job changes to expect after age forty-two, but with increasing life expectancy, the number could easily double to twenty-two or more total jobs in a lifetime!

What is certain is that two essential skill sets will remain at the top of the list of job requirements for 21st century work:

- The ability to quickly acquire and apply new knowledge
- The know-how to apply essential 21st century skills—problem solving, communication, teamwork, technology use, innovation, and the rest—to each and every project, the primary unit of 21st century work

To get a better sense of the rising importance learning and education are playing in our lives today, it's useful to step back and take a look at the roles education has played in the past, where learning is heading, and the forces driving these changes.

Learning Through Time

Currently, nearly 1.5 billion children attend primary and secondary schools in the world—around 77 percent of all school-age children.[5]

A billion and a half schoolchildren is a staggering number, even though it leaves out another three hundred million and more worldwide—most of them girls—who have no access to basic education. Still, just imagine, as the sun rises across each time zone, all those mothers and fathers waking up their children, making sure they are washed and appropriately dressed, have (hopefully) eaten some breakfast, and have gotten off to school on time—each and every day of the school year!

But why is education so important that virtually every country in the world has implemented some sort of formal education system? Why has the United Nations declared it a fundamental right of all children?[6]

And what do parents, teachers, businesses, social institutions, governments, and society as a whole expect from education? Have these expectations changed over time?

The answers to these questions can help us understand what the proper role and purpose of education ought to be in our own times.

Education's Purpose: Historical Roles and Goals

It has been observed that today's education systems operate on an agrarian calendar (summers off to allow students to work in the fields), an industrial time clock (fifty-minute classroom periods marked by bells), and a list of curriculum subjects invented in the Middle Ages (language, math, science, and the arts). It's useful to take a brief look at how this came about and what education's role has been in ages past, before turning to what education means for us now and in the future.

What do a one-room school in a rural farming village, a crowded classroom in a bustling industrial city, and a shiny new school in a high-tech suburban zone have in common? What do we expect them to do for our children? What have we expected from our schools through time?

Education plays four universal roles on society's evolving stage. It empowers us to contribute to work and society, exercise and develop our personal talents, fulfill our civic responsibilities, and carry our traditions and values forward. These are the "great expectations," the big returns we want from our investments in education. Or put another way, these are the four universal goals we expect the education of our children to achieve.

These four pillars of education's purpose remain constant through time—much like psychologist Abraham Maslow's universal "hierarchy of needs," which starts with physical needs and moves up through safety and social needs, then respect and knowledge, and culminates in self-realization and self-transcendence.[7]

But how people go about meeting these four universal needs in different times and ages varies tremendously, as shown in Table 1.2.

In the Agrarian Age, when farming the land was the primary work of society (as it still is in many parts of the world), contributing to society meant learning how to grow food for more than your family. Passing on the knowledge, traditions, and crafts of rural life to your children was an essential survival need. Children worked in the fields next to their parents and other family members, and education beyond farming skills was not a high priority. Civic responsibilities revolved around doing what you could to help your neighbors and others in your village when they were in need, as they would in turn help you when you were in need. The social compact was simple and practical.

In the Industrial Age, when the population dramatically shifted from farm to city and work moved from the fields to the factories, education played new roles in society. Typically, men had one or two career paths: working in a trade, factory, or clerical job, or becoming a manager, administrator, or professional if they could make the grade. Women's choices were, of course, far fewer.

The real challenge for industry was to train as many factory and trade workers as possible. So standardization, uniformity, and mass production were important to both the factory and the classroom. Those few destined for managerial or professional work were given special learning opportunities to develop their potential.

Engineering and science skills, the new engines for industrial growth, were particularly prized, along with the management and financial skills necessary to keep the industrial complex running

Table 1.2. Society's Educational Goals Throughout the Ages.

Goals for Education	Agrarian Age	Industrial Age	Knowledge Age
Contribute to work and society	Grow food for family and others	Serve society through a specialized profession	Contribute to global information and knowledge work
	Create tools and crafts for basic needs	Apply engineering and science to contribute to industrial progress	Innovate new services to meet needs and solve problems
	Participate in the local cottage economy	Contribute one piece of a long chain of production and distribution	Participate in the global economy
Exercise and develop personal talents	Learn the basic 3Rs (reading, 'riting, and 'rithmetic), if possible	Achieve basic literacy and numeracy (for as many people as possible)	Enhance personal development with technology-powered knowledge and productivity tools
	Learn farming and craft skills	Learn factory, trade, and industry job skills (for most people)	Take advantage of expanded global opportunities for knowledge work and entrepreneurship as middle class grows
	Use tools to create useful artifacts	Learn managerial and administrative skills, engineering, and science (for a few at the top)	Use knowledge tools and technology to continue learning and developing talents throughout life
Fulfill civic responsibilities	Help neighbors	Participate in social and civic organizations to benefit the community	Participate in community decision making and political activity online and in person
	Contribute to local village needs	Participate in organized labor and political activities	Engage globally in issues through online communities and social networks
	Support essential local services and community celebrations	Contribute to local and regional civic improvement through volunteering and philanthropy	Use communication and social networking tools to contribute time and resources to both local and global causes

Table 1.2.   Society's Educational Goals Throughout the Ages, *continued*

Goals for Education	Agrarian Age	Industrial Age	Knowledge Age
Carry traditions and values forward	Pass on farming knowledge and traditions to the next generation	Learn the past knowledge of a trade, craft, or profession and pass this on to the next generation	Quickly learn traditional knowledge in a field and apply its principles across other fields to create new knowledge and innovations
	Raise children in the ethnic, religious, and cultural traditions of parents and ancestors	Maintain one's own culture and values amid a diversity of traditions in urban life	Build identity from and compassion for a wide range of cultures and traditions
		Connect with other cultures and geographies as communication and transportation expand	Participate in a wide diversity of traditions and multicultural experiences
			Blend traditions and global citizenship into new traditions and values to pass on

smoothly. And with the great mixing of cultures in urban centers, people became more aware (and eventually more tolerant) of traditions different from their own.

Education's Role in the 21st Century

This brings us to our own time, our recently arrived Knowledge Age. In our newly flat world of connected knowledge work, global markets, tele-linked citizens, and blended cultural traditions, the 21st century demands a fresh set of responses.[8] (See Table 1.2.) In the Knowledge Age, brainpower replaces brawnpower, and mechanical horsepower gives way to electronic hertzpower.

Achieving education's goals in our times is shaped by the increasingly powerful technologies we have for communicating, collaborating, and learning. And learning assumes a central role throughout life.

Contributing to Work and Society   To be a productive contributor to society in our 21st century, you need to be able to quickly learn the core content of a field of knowledge while also mastering a broad portfolio of essential learning, innovation, technology, and career skills needed for work and life. And when you apply these skills to today's knowledge and innovation work, you are participating in a global network in which, for example, a product may be designed in California, manufactured in China, assembled in the Czech Republic, and sold in chain stores in cities across the world.

This global network of economic, technological, political, social, and ecological interconnections is no less than breathtaking. We work with the support of multiple teams spread across the world to get things done, solve problems, and create and deliver new services. But since our interlinked economies depend on both natural and human resources from around the globe, we must continually find new ways to preserve our natural world while building more harmonious, culturally rich, and creative societies.

Fulfilling Personal Talents   With only 77 percent of the world's school-age children currently in school, we have a long way to go to reach universal access to a basic education. But countries are stepping up their investments in education as an economic imperative, and as a result, more students are gaining more opportunities to develop their talents.

Today nearly two billion cell phones are in use around the world, and access to the Internet is rapidly increasing in schools, homes, community centers, and Internet cafés worldwide. This is providing even more opportunities to learn and develop skills.

As amplifiers, storerooms, and sensory extensions for our thinking and communicating, digital devices and the Internet are today's power tools for building abilities and sharing talents. Making these tools universally accessible and closing the digital divide between the information rich and the information poor will provide more opportunities for learners to realize their potential. People everywhere will then be able to contribute their own special talents and gifts to the health and welfare of their community, the economy, and to society as a whole.

Fulfilling Civic Responsibilities   With access to the expanded spectrum of issues, facts, opinions, and conversations that our increasingly media-rich and Internet-connected world brings us, our potential for informed participation in democratic decision making has never been better. E-mail, the Internet, and cell phones have made it easier to connect with others who share our interests and concerns and to coordinate our social, civic, and community activities.

At the same time, the potential for information overload, distraction, and analysis paralysis when facing demands for attention from too many sources—ranging from well-informed and reliable to woefully uninformed and even deliberately misleading—is also high. Learning to manage our digital power tools and to apply the critical thinking and information literacy skills needed to put all this information to good use is a clear challenge for the 21st century.

As the campaign and presidency of the world's first Internet president, Barack Obama, has shown, technology can be a powerful tool for personally engaging citizens in the political issues of our times and in the process of change. In many ways, we are just beginning to understand how to tap the enormous power of online social technologies for collaborative problem solving, political action, and community building.

Carrying Forward Traditions and Values   Learning the core principles and traditions of a field of knowledge and blending these with the knowledge and practices of other fields to invent and introduce new knowledge, new services, and new products, will be a high-demand skill set in the 21st century.

Increased mobility, immigration, intermarriage, and access to job opportunities worldwide have led to another kind of blending and mixing—communities across the globe are becoming ever more culturally diverse. Though this diversity has brought vitality and richness to our communities, differences between traditional culture and modern values are still a troubling source of tension in the world.

The 21st century challenge for each of us is to build and maintain our own identity from our given traditions and from the wide variety of traditions all around us. At the same time we must all learn to apply tolerance and compassion for the different identities and values of others.

With the growing diversity of global traditions and values that now surrounds us, the challenge to maintaining social harmony is great, but the opportunities for richer, more creative, and vibrant communities are even greater.

Our historic shift to a 21st century Knowledge Age, decades in the making, has forever tilted the balance of what is needed and valued in our work, our learning, and our life. In the 21st century, lifelong learning is here to stay.

Fortunately, a number of powerful global forces are coming together to help transform learning to meet the demands of our times.

2

The Perfect Learning Storm

FOUR CONVERGING FORCES

Automobiles are cultural icons of modern times. How cars have been designed and manufactured in the past decades can reveal just how much times have changed, as the historical fiction tale in the sidebar "Shifting Through Three Generations" illustrates.

Anita, Peter, Lee . . . three generations working, learning, and living in ways that reflect their times. So what are the societal forces that make Lee's world so different from that of his father or his grandmother? And how are these changing forces reshaping our learning, work, and life in the 21st century?

As shown in Figure 2.1, four powerful forces are converging and leading us toward new ways of learning for life in the 21st century:

- Knowledge work
- Thinking tools
- Digital lifestyles
- Learning research

These four forces are simultaneously creating the need for new forms of learning in the 21st century and supplying the tools,

Shifting Through Three Generations

Anita spent most of her working life on the auto assembly line installing interior dome lights. It was tedious and noisy work, but through the 1940s and '50s she earned enough money to help put her son, Peter, through college. Though she never went to college herself, she had high hopes that education would bring him a better life.

As a child, Peter was fascinated by robots—he loved science fiction movies, comic books, and, of course, cars. He studied mechanical engineering at the nearby university, did well, and eventually landed a job designing and later maintaining robotic assembly arms for the same auto plant where his mother worked.

Anita proudly joked that her son was "replacing her with a robot." As the plant continued to automate routine tasks through the 1980s and early '90s, it offered fewer routine jobs like Anita's and many more highly skilled jobs like Peter's.

Peter's son, Lee, always loved animals and nature. He also liked tinkering in his dad's shop creating new habitats for his pet hamsters, turtles, and fish. As a design student in college, he became an active environmentalist committed to designing environmentally sound products, and especially, to "greening" the automobile industry that was so much a part of his family's life.

In late 2008, when the global financial crisis hit the auto industry hard and even Peter had to look for a new job, Lee managed to find work with a brand new start-up, Suncar, designing components for plug-in hybrid cars charged by solar panels.

Lee's work now, as in most start-up businesses, is both very exciting and very demanding—he often works late into the night. Coordinating his project work online with a design team spread across the world is a real challenge. But Lee knows this is the future. He is committed to designing the best "green" car in the world and to making the world a greener and healthier place to live.

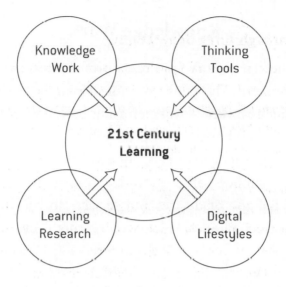

Figure 2.1. 21st Century Learning Convergence.

environments, and guiding principles required to support 21st century learning practices.

In the three-generation historical sketch in the sidebar, it's easy to see how these forces have been emerging to transform work and learning. From Anita to Peter to Lee, each generation was increasingly surrounded by more digital devices, each had to use more advanced technologies and more collaborative ways of working, and work became increasingly less routine and manual, and more abstract, knowledge-based, and design-oriented.

Today, in Lee's time, recent cognitive and neuroscience research in how human beings actually learn and develop is beginning to reshape education and training in schools and at work around the world.

This chapter gives you a closer look at each of these converging forces and their impact on learning today and tomorrow.

Knowledge Work

As noted, the 21st century has already brought historic changes to the world of work. The Knowledge Age demands a steady supply of well-trained workers—workers using brainpower and digital tools to apply well-honed knowledge skills to their daily work.

Today's knowledge work is done collaboratively in teams, with team members often spread across multiple locations, using a digital zoo of devices and services to coordinate their project work: cell phones, Voice over Internet Protocol communications, teleconferencing, Web conferencing, laptops, personal digital assistants, databases, spreadsheets, calendar and contact management software, e-mail, text messaging, Web sites, online collaboration spaces, social networking tools—the list goes on and on.

The need for knowledge workers to create and innovate new products and services that solve real problems and meet the needs of real customers is a major driving force for economic growth and work in the 21st century.

Shortages of well-trained workers, especially in the technical areas of science, technology, engineering, and mathematics (the so-called STEM subjects) are a growing concern among business leaders. This demand has led to a brisk global talent trade and to heated controversies over practices such as bringing in skilled foreign workers on special visas and outsourcing work to lower-wage countries such as India and China.

Many high-tech corporations are also making substantial investments in global programs to attract students to technical fields and to train and certify them in technical skills. Some multinational corporations are now investing in the professional development of teachers and the digital outfitting of schools around the globe, so that the pipeline for future knowledge workers will be full and flowing fast.

In short, pressure is increasing on education systems around the world to teach in ways that will produce the knowledge workers and innovators businesses need to be successful in the 21st century knowledge economy.

Thinking Tools

Technology and the digital devices and services that fill a knowledge worker's toolkit—the thinking tools of our time—may be the most potent forces for change in the 21st century. The speed at which the underlying information and communications technologies are developing is truly astounding:

- Computer microchips continue to double their processing speed every eighteen months. The average cell phone has more processing power than all the computers used to plan and run the early space missions.[1]
- The density of data we can store doubles every twelve months. The 140 million books, photographs, movies, and other documents of the U.S. Library of Congress can now fit on a single digital tape cassette.[2]
- The amount of information we can transmit over optical fibers doubles every nine months. All the books ever written can be transmitted over an optical fiber the width of your hair in just a couple of seconds.[3]

With the mushrooming capacity to process, store, and transmit the bits and bytes of information, we are rapidly gaining fingertip access to much of the world's available information. For example, in July 2008 Google announced that it had reached a new milestone: one trillion Web pages indexed for use by its Internet search engine. Some predict that by 2010 the amount of new technical knowledge will double every seventy-two hours.[4]

With these waves of information and knowledge crashing all around them, how are today's students going to manage and learn from this deluge?

In the past, memorizing the tidy set of known facts, rules, figures, and dates of any school subject was a challenging but necessary part of learning. Today, attempting to memorize the overflowing storerooms of facts and knowledge in any field is clearly impossible. But an immense number of facts can be "remembered" or accessed as needed with a quick Internet search.

Yet knowing a field's core ideas, understanding its fundamental principles, and applying this knowledge to solve new problems and answer new questions are evergreen learning tasks that will never become outdated. These learning skills need to move to the heart of what our schools teach.

Thinking and knowledge tools are helping us learn, work, and be creative. But they entail a host of downsides: the beeps and fanfares of cell phones; the flood of e-mail, text messages, and "tweets" to answer (and spam and other advertising messages to plough through); the dozens of file formats and endless software updates to juggle; along with software crashes, privacy concerns, identity theft, and on and on. In addition, quantity of information is not the same as quality. Much of what is available to us is rumor, personal opinion, marketing copy disguised as Web content, or otherwise unreliable material.

Nonetheless, as technology continues to improve, the benefits our digital tools bring seem to far outweigh the drawbacks. The mental tasks of knowledge work—accessing, searching, analyzing, storing, managing, creating, and communicating information and knowledge—are becoming easier and more efficient as our digital tools for thinking, learning, communicating, collaborating, and working become more powerful, integrated, connected, and easier to use. These 21st century companions are helping more and more of us meet the demands of our times effectively and creatively.

Digital Lifestyles

Whether you call them "digital natives," "net geners," "netizens," "homo zappiens," or something else, it is clear that the members of the first generation to grow up surrounded by digital media (those now aged eleven to thirty-one) are different from the "digital immigrants" who learned to "do technology" later in life.[5]

In 1975, for example, the average home media environment included four "information products" (TV programming, news, advertising, and radio programming) delivered by only five routes (broadcast TV and radio, phone, mail, newspaper delivery). Display and listening devices were limited to TVs, radios, stereos, telephones, and paper. And storage options ranged from paper to vinyl records to tape, whether reel-to-reel, eight-track, or cassette.[6]

Today, each of these categories holds two to four times as many items. Consider the following innovations that have come into common use since 1975:

Cable TV	Instant messaging
Camcorders	Internet (Web sites, blogs,
CDs and DVDs	newsgroups, chat)
Cell phones (including	iPods and MP3 players
iPhones, BlackBerrys)	Memory sticks
Digital video recorders	Online storage
DVD players and drives	PDAs
e-Book readers	Personal and laptop computers
E-mail	Satellite TV and radio
Game consoles	Text messaging
Hard drives	VCRs

This list was no doubt incomplete as soon as it was written—the pace of new digital devices coming into the market (and leaving it) is overwhelming. And the variety of ways these devices can now interconnect in a home's digital ecology is even more bewildering.

A moment's reflection will reveal another difference between 1975 and today. Then, devices tended to have a single use, and you had few choices for how and where you could take in content (the audio, video, or print). Paper media—newspapers and magazines—were as versatile as you could get. Today, TV, music, online content, traditional print, and personal communications can all be delivered, watched, heard, or read on multiple portable devices.

No wonder net geners are different from their parents, having grown up "bathed in bits" since they were born.[7] But there is more to it than their heightened abilities to multitask, search the Web, listen to music, update their blogs, create Web sites, make movies, play video games, and text friends on their cell phones. These young people are the first generation in history to know more about the most powerful tools for change in our society—digital information and communications technologies—than their elders: their parents and teachers. This is changing both family and school dynamics, as students switch roles and become digital mentors, and teachers and parents become part-time students of our young digital experts.

Net geners' lifelong immersion in all things digital has given them a whole new set of desires and expectations. In a recent study of more than eleven thousand individuals aged eleven to thirty-one, eight common attitudes, behaviors, and expectations were found that clearly distinguish them from their parents.[8] They want (and more than their predecessors of the 1960s, *expect*) the following:

- Freedom to choose what's right for them and to express their personal views and individual identity
- Customization and personalization, the ability to change things to better suit their own needs
- Scrutiny—detailed, behind-the-scenes analysis so they can find out what the real story is
- Integrity and openness in their interactions with others and from organizations like businesses, government, and educational institutions

- Entertainment and play to be integrated into their work, learning, and social life
- Collaboration and relationships to be a vital part of all they do
- Speed in communications, getting information, and getting responses to questions and messages
- Innovation in products, services, employers, and schools, and in their own lives

These net gen expectations present new sets of demands on our education systems—demands that are coming from education's clients and customers—the growing ranks of net generation students.

A one-size-fits-all factory model and one-way broadcast approach to learning does not work well for these students. New ways to make learning interactive, personalized, collaborative, creative, and innovative are needed to engage and keep net geners actively learning in schools everywhere.

Learning Research

The last three decades have brought an important revolution in our understanding of how people learn. This new "learning about learning" is surprisingly in tune with both the new expectations of net generation students and the new demands and tools of the Knowledge Age.[9]

As discussed in the following sections, five key findings from research in the science of learning can be used to direct and guide our efforts to reshape learning to meet our times:[10]

- Authentic learning
- Mental model building
- Internal motivation
- Multiple intelligences
- Social learning

Authentic Learning

Context, or the conditions in which learning activities occur (the people, objects, symbols, and environment and how they all work together to support learning), are much more influential than previously thought.[11]

Transferring what is learned from one context to another (such as from the classroom to the real world) is often not successful. Doing supermarket math problems on a test is different from mentally calculating price differences of three kinds and sizes of laundry soap in an actual store. The setting in which a new skill or piece of knowledge is learned strongly influences whether or not that skill or knowledge can be applied elsewhere.

Simulating the real-world environment with media or by actually being in a place where that particular skill or knowledge is used in the world—supplying a more authentic context for learning—increases the chance that a lesson will be remembered and can be used in other similar situations.[12]

This finding suggests students need more real-world problem solving, internships or apprenticeships in real work settings, and other more authentic learning experiences to make learning last and be useful.

Mental Model Building

A great deal has been learned about how people build mental models, incorporate new experiences into these models, and change these models over time.[13] We all start with less than accurate mental models of the world based on our experience *(the Earth sure looks flat to me)* and adjust them as we encounter new experiences that don't quite fit *(wow, the Earth looks like a giant floating blue-and-white marble in those photos from space)*. The building and changing of our mental models, and how we link our mental models together in our heads—our shifting systems view of the world—is much of what learning is all about.[14]

Recognizing what you already know from past experience—and what you currently believe from the latest versions of your mental models—are important first steps in the learning process. Unfortunately, in our haste to teach new material, the important step of helping learners reflect on their current mental models is often overlooked.[15]

Building and manipulating external models, whether they're physical ones (wood or LEGO blocks, robotic parts, and the like) or virtual ones (drawings on paper or screens, computer simulations like The Sims or Spore, virtual worlds like Second Life, video games, and so on) help us visualize and further develop our internal mental models.

Both *visceral* (hands-on) and *virtual* (on-screen) modeling activities provide ways to make thinking visible, reflecting the internal model making and learning going on inside our heads.[16]

Internal Motivation

A rich literature of emotional intelligence studies and reports are clearly showing the advantages of being internally motivated to learn, as opposed to learning just for external motivations such as parental approval or performance on tests.[17] When people have an emotional connection to what is being learned—a personal experience or question—learning can be sustained longer, understanding can become deeper, and what is learned can be retained longer.[18] Studies of well-designed learning projects geared to student interests and passions also show that internal motivation can contribute a great deal to active engagement, deeper understanding, and a desire to learn more.[19]

Multiple Intelligences

Though a lively debate continues over what exactly are the inherent "parts of intelligence" in the brain,[20] there is no question now that competence comes in a variety of forms and intelligence is exhibited in a wide assortment of behaviors. Encouraging multiple learning approaches to match diverse learning styles and providing multiple ways for students to express their understanding is necessary for effective learning.[21]

How to personalize learning and how to differentiate instruction for diverse classrooms are two of the great educational challenges of the 21st century. The evidence is clear that personalized learning can have a positive effect on both learning performance and attitudes toward learning.[22]

With recent developments in learning technology such as the Universal Design for Learning approach and tools,[23] we can now begin to personalize learning to meet each student's learning abilities and disabilities, learning styles and preferences, and unique profile of talents and competence.

Social Learning

In many ways, all learning is social, in that it is based on the accumulated knowledge gained by scores of others down through the ages. Even the solitary reading of a book or Web page is actually a social act that puts you in touch with all the people who influenced the author's thinking and writing.

Both face-to-face and virtual collaborations online have been shown to increase learning motivation, create better and more innovative results, and develop social and cross-cultural skills.[24] Learning in a community of learners who share knowledge, questions, skills, progress, and passion for a subject is exactly how adults learn when they participate in their communities of work and professional practice.[25]

A wide variety of online communication tools and environments that support social, collaborative, and community approaches to learning are now available. Since the Internet is global, students can now be global learners, connecting and learning with others around the planet.

The Forces of Resistance

Knowledge work, thinking tools, digital lifestyles, and learning research are all coming together in what appears to be a "perfect learning storm," ushering in new ways of learning (a topic we return to in Chapter Seven). Although these combined forces for a 21st century model of learning are powerful and growing, a number of forces are still resisting these changes:

- Industrial Age education policies designed to deliver mass education as efficiently as possible (which worked well until times changed).
- Educational accountability and standardized testing systems that primarily measure performance on basic skills such as reading and math (but currently skip measures of 21st century skills).
- The sheer momentum of decades (or possibly centuries) of teaching practices based on transmitting knowledge to students through direct instruction (despite the growing ranks of teachers worldwide who would like more training in how to help their students construct and apply knowledge through discovery, exploration, and project learning methods).
- The combined weight of the educational publishing industry, which still makes much of its income on textbook sales (as much as individual companies might like to move to a flexible, all-digital approach to educational content).
- The fear among some educational organizations that hard-sought improvements in traditional learning outcomes

through a focus on rigorous content will be undermined by a new focus on skills (though it is widely understood that content knowledge and skills always work together—that is, you can't think critically or communicate about nothing!).

- The preferences of parents, who as children learned through traditional approaches and as adults have been successful in their own careers, to have their children learn in the same ways they did. Often they want their children to succeed on the same kinds of tests and exams they took when they were in school and are reluctant to see their schools experimenting with changes that might jeopardize their children's success (and do not quite see the association between the need for new learning methods that teach the 21st century skills and the skills they use in their everyday work, though they would also like their children to have these skills).

Despite these and other strong resistive pressures, the global convergence of forces for change toward a 21st century learning model are gradually winning out. More and more schools and communities are adopting 21st century learning approaches each year. We are accelerating toward a new balance for 21st century education.

The Turning of Learning: Toward a New Balance

Singapore is well known for its success in modernizing its education system and for the high levels of academic performance students achieve there. Yet it has much more to accomplish in its transformation to a 21st century learning system.

Tay Lai Ling, the deputy director for Curriculum Policy and Pedagogy for the Singapore Ministry of Education, puts it this way:

> We have come a long way in changing our teaching and learning methods, but our teachers and students still have farther to go. We have a new slogan at the Ministry that will hopefully encourage further change.
>
> The slogan is "Teach Less, Learn More."

Bob Pearlman, director of Strategic Planning for the New Tech Foundation, a fast-growing network of project learning high schools, echoes both the excitement and the challenge in making 21st century learning a reality:

> New Technology Foundation takes its mission statement seriously: "To re-invent teaching and learning for the 21st century." It's a tremendous challenge, especially finding teachers and then training, coaching, and supporting them to develop effective projects that help each student build knowledge and understanding, basic and 21st century skills, at the same time. But it's working for kids from all walks of life, urban, suburban, and rural, and most of New Tech's work is with students from less privileged backgrounds. I can't think of anything more important than preparing all our students to succeed in the real world.

What are these schools doing to shift their balance toward 21st century learning? What does this shifting balance look like? What does this mean for teachers and students in school classrooms each day?

Figure 2.2 lists ranges of teaching and learning practices. As education adapts learning methods to meet the demands of the 21st century, schools, districts, states, provinces, education departments, and ministries all over the world are shifting their practices toward a new balance, leaning more to the right of the range of each of these practices.

Take a moment to think about all the new 21st century demands on education. We face demands from the new global knowledge economy; from the converging forces of knowledge work, digital tools, and lifestyles; from modern learning research;

Teacher-directed	Learner-centered
Direct instruction	Interactive exchange
Knowledge	Skills
Content	Process
Basic skills	Applied skills
Facts and principles	Questions and problems
Theory	Practice
Curriculum	Projects
Time-slotted	On-demand
One-size-fits-all	Personalized
Competitive	Collaborative
Classroom	Global community
Text-based	Web-based
Summative tests	Formative evaluations
Learning for school	Learning for life

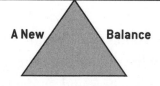

A New Balance

Figure 2.2. 21st Century Learning Balance.

and from the need for the skills most in demand in our times: problem-solving, being creative and innovative, communicating, collaborating, being flexible, and so on.

Then look at the learning balance chart in Figure 2.2 and ask yourself—can we really prepare our students with just the left side of the chart of learning practices alone? These have been the prevailing teaching and learning methods for quite some time. But will they really prepare our students for success in this new century?

It is important to understand that the learning practices indicated by the two terms in each pair are not yes-no, either-or educational choices. Each line represents a both-and spectrum—a continuum of learning practices blending both approaches. For instance, focusing on applied skills and learning processes doesn't mean you abandon the teaching of basic skills or the learning of content knowledge and facts. The two must work hand in hand, in the right balance for each learner. Becoming competent in any subject area means developing both the knowledge and the skills to apply that knowledge to the kinds of questions and problems experts in that field would tackle.

Teachers who are shifting their practices to meet the needs of our times talk about how they're remixing the coverage of content with the uncovering of ideas and concepts, and how they're rebalancing their time between being the "sage on the stage," who presents, explains, and answers questions and the "guide on the side," who supports students' research, discovery, and sharing of their own findings in learning projects.

As one teacher put it, "I had to unlearn the idea that teaching was about *my* content; I had to learn it was about *their* thinking and *their* skills."

Digital technologies are increasingly supporting many of the learning approaches on both sides of the balance. They are boosting basic skills such as the recall of math principles and procedures, vocabulary development in language, and internalization of science terms and principles. Learning technologies are also freeing up time to focus on the 21st century skills that require more interaction among learners while providing tools to further their skill-building online—collaboration, communication, leadership, and social and cross-cultural skills.

Clearly it will take the best from the entire range of learning practices represented to successfully prepare our students for their future, with the approaches on the right side of the chart becoming more and more important as we move through our century. The educational balance is shifting, and a new teaching and learning balance is evolving in schools around the globe that better meets the demands of our times and the times to come. We explore these new practices further in Part Three of the book, the "how" of 21st century learning. But first, in Part Two, we look at the kinds of skills students will need to develop to succeed in the 21st century.

The Top 21st Century Challenge

Education's big goal, preparing students to contribute to the world of work and civic life, has become one of our century's biggest challenges. In fact, all the other great problems of our times—solving global warming, curing diseases, ending poverty, and the rest—don't stand a chance without education preparing each citizen to play a part in helping to solve our collective problems.

Learning for work and life in our times means helping as many children as possible learn to apply 21st century skills and a solid understanding of core subjects to the challenges of our times.

A 21st century education for every child is the first challenge— the one that will enable all our other challenges to be met.

| **PART TWO** |

WHAT ARE 21ST CENTURY SKILLS?

3

Learning and Innovation Skills

LEARNING TO CREATE TOGETHER

In times past, education was primarily focused on learning the important content for each subject area, then assessing this content knowledge with quizzes and tests at the end of a lesson. So in science, for instance, a student might first study the periodic table of elements, then take a test on what H, Na, Cl, Fe (hydrogen, sodium, chlorine, and iron) and other element symbols stand for, how they are arranged in the table, and other related information.

The P21 learning framework expands and deepens this earlier model, making it more suited to our times. First the traditional core subject areas that are taught in most schools today usually include reading, writing, language arts (in the native language), world languages (second or third language), mathematics, science, the arts, social studies and geography, government and civics, and history. Then come the 21st century subject themes, such as financial, health, and environmental literacy, then the three sets of skills most needed in the 21st century.

Before going into the details, take a look at the sidebar titled "The SARS Project"—yes, *that* SARS as in Severe Acute Respiratory Syndrome—to see an example of the new framework in action.

The SARS Project

The SARS Web site (shown in Figure 3.1; available for viewing at http://library.thinkquest.org/03oct/00738/) is the result of a real student project that illustrates just how powerful learning can be when it is driven by a real-world problem and by a learning design that naturally builds most of the 21st century skills discussed here and in the next two chapters.

Each year student teams from all over the world compete in a well-known competition called ThinkQuest (www.thinkquest.org). The challenge is to create an innovative educational Web site for use by other students on a topic the team really cares about.

In 2003, six high school students—Kian Huat from Kuala Lumpur, Malaysia; Ming Han from Singapore; Barthe and Jorrit (twins) from Veghel, the Netherlands; Ahmed from Cairo; and Van from Philadelphia—collaborated online to create a site on a topic of great concern at the time—the deadly outbreak of the Severe Acute Respiratory Syndrome, or SARS, virus.

The global team of students had to do all the work involved in producing an engaging educational Web site: researching the topic, interviewing experts, writing the text, designing and creating the look and feel of the site (the layout of text, images, illustrations, animations, and videos), and programming the site's interface, navigation, interactive games, and quizzes. The geographic dispersion of the team, and the vastly different time zones they lived in, made the use of online tools to plan, schedule, communicate, and coordinate all of their work essential.

We refer to the SARS project often to provide concrete examples of how students develop each of the 21st century skills. The project is documented in a video on the DVD included with this book and available online at this book's Web site (http://21stcenturyskillsbook.com), as well as on the Oracle Education Foundation's Web site (http://www.oraclefoundation.org/single_player.html?v=2).

DVD

Take a moment to watch the video and view the award-winning student Web site.

Figure 3.1. SARS Web Site Screenshot.

The Knowledge-and-Skills Rainbow

Throughout the next few chapters, and a number of times in the rest of the book, we will be referring to the "21st Century Knowledge-and-Skills Rainbow," which makes up half of the P21 learning framework (see Appendix B for details on the Partnership for 21st Century Skills and its 21st Century Learning Framework). The rainbow illustrates the desired student outcomes most needed for our times including learning through traditional school subjects and contemporary content themes, combined with 21st century skills. The framework adds to the traditional subjects interdisciplinary 21st century themes relevant to some of the key issues and problems of our times, such as global awareness (multicultural awareness and understanding); environmental literacy (ecological awareness and understanding of energy and resource sustainability); financial literacy (economic, business, and entrepreneurial knowledge); health literacy (health care, nutrition, and preventive medicine); and civic literacy (civic engagement, community service, ethics, and social justice).

Finally, the core subjects and interdisciplinary 21st century themes are surrounded by the three sets of skills most in demand in the 21st century:

- Learning and innovation skills
- Information, media, and technology skills
- Life and career skills

Figure 3.2 shows the structure and components of the rainbow—the skills, knowledge, and expertise students need to master to work and live successfully in the 21st century.

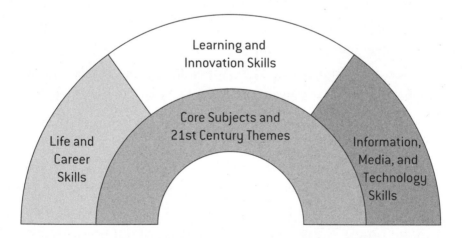

Figure 3.2. The 21st Century Knowledge-and-Skills Rainbow.

Learning to Learn and Innovate

The first set of 21st century skills focuses on critical learning skills and innovation:

- Critical thinking and problem solving (expert thinking)
- Communication and collaboration (complex communicating)
- Creativity and innovation (applied imagination and invention)

These skills are the keys to unlocking a lifetime of learning and creative work. As described in Chapter One, the new world of work is demanding ever higher levels of expert thinking and complex communicating.[1] The first two skills in this set, critical thinking and problem solving, and communication and collaboration, are the key learning and knowledge work skills that address these new work skill demands.

The 21st century global economy is also requiring higher levels of imagination, creativity, and innovation to continually invent new and better services and products for the global marketplace. Thus the third skill, creativity and innovation, focuses on discovery and invention.

Beyond meeting the new demands of 21st century work, these three skills have long been at the heart of what it takes to become a self-reliant lifelong learner. The ability to ask and answer important questions, to critically review what others say about a subject, to pose and solve problems, to communicate and work with others in learning, and to create new knowledge and innovations that help build a better world—these have always been at the core of learning and innovation. So we have both timeless universal reasons and urgent practical needs to put these three skill sets on the top of the 21st century skills list.

But what is involved in learning each of these skills?

Critical Thinking and Problem Solving

Critical thinking and problem solving are considered by many to be the new basics of 21st century learning. Recent research in *cognition,* the science of thinking, has punctured a time-honored tenet of teaching—that mastering content must come before an attempt to put it to good use. As it turns out, using knowledge as it is being learned—applying skills like critical thinking, problem solving, and creativity to the content knowledge—increases motivation and improves learning outcomes.

As Lauren Resnick and Megan Hall, internationally known scholars in the cognitive science of learning and instruction, have written, "What we know now is that just as facts do not constitute true knowledge and thinking power, so thinking processes cannot proceed without something to think about."[2]

In every subject, at every grade level, instruction and learning must include commitment to a knowledge core, high demands on thinking, and active use of knowledge.[3]

What's more, the lockstep, one-before-the-other learning sequence that teachers have been taught in education schools and enshrined in the famous "Taxonomy for Learning"[4]—first *knowledge,* then *comprehension,* then *application,* then *analysis,* then *synthesis,* and finally *evaluation*—has been shattered by decades of accumulated research that proves this is not how students really learn most effectively—or in many cases, not how they learn at all.[5]

The revised version of the taxonomy uses the updated terms *remember, understand, apply, analyze, evaluate,* and *create,* and it provides definitive proof that, as the authors point out, "these processes can be learned at the same time or even in reverse order."[6] Furthermore, research has shown that combining many of these thinking skills improves learning outcomes. Creating, applying, remembering, analyzing, understanding, and evaluating can all be used together in rich, well-designed learning activities and projects to improve the effectiveness and longevity of learning results.

In the SARS project, all of these thinking and learning skills were applied. The student team was confronted with an immense amount of content knowledge, including the biology of the SARS virus, the medical reports on the virus's effects on the body, the most effective methods to prevent and treat the disease, the mathematical and epidemiological data on the spread of the disease, and the social and governmental responses to monitoring and controlling the outbreak.

The team's challenge was to use their critical thinking skills—the ability to analyze, interpret, evaluate, summarize, and synthesize all this information—and apply the results to solve an urgent problem: getting other students to overcome their fears by learning more about the disease and about ways to protect themselves from the viral outbreak. The project team had to present the results

Critical Thinking and Problem Solving Skills

Students should be able to:

Reason effectively

- Use various types of reasoning (inductive, deductive, etc.) as appropriate to the situation

Use systems thinking

- Analyze how parts of a whole interact with each other to produce overall outcomes in complex systems

Make judgments and decisions

- Effectively analyze and evaluate evidence, arguments, claims and beliefs
- Analyze and evaluate major alternative points of view
- Synthesize and make connections between information and arguments
- Interpret information and draw conclusions based on the best analysis
- Reflect critically on learning experiences and processes

Solve problems

- Solve different kinds of nonfamiliar problems in both conventional and innovative ways
- Identify and ask significant questions that clarify various points of view and lead to better solutions

Source: Copyright © Partnership for 21st Century Skills. Reprinted by permission of the Partnership for 21st Century Skills, www.21stcenturyskills.org.

of its research in a way that appealed to other students, engaging their interest through images, animations, video, and interactive games, as well as through clear and concise writing.

Many of the skills the SARS team used are also the key components, or subskills, of the critical thinking and problem-solving skills outlined in the P21 Framework. The team members used their reasoning skills to present a clear and logical story of how the SARS outbreak started and spread. They made sound judgments and decisions on what was credible and what was unreliable information, based on thorough analyses and evaluations of the medical and sociological evidence and various expert points of view. The students applied a systems approach to analyzing the complex, interrelated factors in the disease's spread and the effectiveness of various prevention methods, and solved a number of design problems in presenting the SARS story effectively, choosing the best methods to communicate their findings to their audience. Through their work on the project, the team members practiced and developed all the important component skills involved in critical thinking and problem solving.

What gives these timeless thinking skills a 21st century twist are the powerful technologies available today for accessing, searching, analyzing, storing, managing, creating, and communicating information to support critical thinking and problem solving. Students can now reach experts by e-mail, text message their learning partners, and work collaboratively to create documents and Web sites online.

Critical thinking and problem-solving skills can be learned through a variety of inquiry and problem-solving activities and programs (see Appendix A). These skills are developed most effectively through meaningful learning projects driven by engaging questions and problems, such as the SARS project. Increasingly complex project challenges can be used to hone these skills over time, as discussed further in Part Three of this book.

Communication and Collaboration

While education has always been concerned with the basics of good communicating—correct speech, fluent reading, and clear writing—digital tools and the demands of our times call for a much wider and deeper personal portfolio of communication and collaboration skills to promote learning together.

In the SARS project, the six student team members, working from four different time zones, exchanged nearly three thousand messages in the course of their project. They used over a dozen different software and Web tools to create and share their work online, constantly adding, editing, and modifying one another's work as they developed their Web site.

The first time they actually met face-to-face was at the Think-Quest Live award event in San Francisco, and even though they had spent countless hours working together online, it took them the better part of a day to fully readjust to each other. There are no accents in online messages, and the finer points of personality, style, body language, and jokes could not be fully appreciated until the team was physically together. By the end of their week together, they understood one another in new ways and could communicate on more meaningful levels. Their friendship also deepened.

Communication and Collaboration Skills

Students should be able to:

Communicate clearly

- Articulate thoughts and ideas effectively using oral, written and nonverbal communication skills in a variety of forms and contexts
- Listen effectively to decipher meaning, including knowledge, values, attitudes and intentions
- Use communication for a range of purposes (e.g., to inform, instruct, motivate and persuade)
- Utilize multiple media and technologies, and know how to judge their effectiveness a priori as well as assess their impact
- Communicate effectively in diverse environments (including multi-lingual)

Collaborate with others

- Demonstrate ability to work effectively and respectfully with diverse teams
- Exercise flexibility and willingness to be helpful in making necessary compromises to accomplish a common goal
- Assume shared responsibility for collaborative work, and value the individual contributions made by each team member

Source: Copyright © Partnership for 21st Century Skills. Reprinted by permission of the Partnership for 21st Century Skills, www.21stcenturyskills.org.

The communication and collaboration skills the SARS team members used in their project are good examples of the sets of subskills that contribute to effective communicating and collaborating. In creating their Web site they had to communicate clearly in their writing and in their visual design, and they had to listen and consider each other's viewpoints to work as an effective team. They designed effective and engaging Web site communication features, and they each collaborated with the other members of their diverse team using a variety of information and communication tools. They applied most of the P21 skills that go into making a proficient 21st century communicator and collaborator.

These skills can be learned through a wide variety of methods, but they are best learned socially—by directly communicating and collaborating with others, either physically, face-to-face, or virtually, through technology. Team learning projects that involve intense communication and collaboration during the course of the project are excellent ways to develop these skills (more on this and other powerful learning methods in Part Three).

Creativity and Innovation

Given the 21st century demands to continuously innovate new services, better processes, and improved products for the world's global economy, and for the creative knowledge work required in more and more of the world's better-paying jobs, it should come as no surprise that creativity and innovation are very high on the list of 21st century skills.

In fact, many believe that our current Knowledge Age is quickly giving way to an Innovation Age, where the ability to solve problems in new ways (like the greening of energy use), to invent new technologies (like bio- and nanotechnology) or create the next killer application of existing technologies (like efficient and affordable electric cars and solar panels), or even to discover new branches of knowledge and invent entirely new industries, will all be highly prized.

Unfortunately, too often, as Sir Kenneth Robinson, a thought leader on creativity, has said, "We do not grow into creativity, we grow out of it—or rather, we are educated out of it." Traditional education's focus on facts, memorization, basic skills, and test taking has not been good for the development of creativity and innovation.[7] This is changing in the 21st century, and education systems from Finland to Singapore are beginning to put creativity and innovation as a high priority in their desired outcomes for student learning.

The lack of attention to developing creativity and innovation skills is partly based on a number of common misconceptions— creativity is only for geniuses, or only for the young, or can't be learned or measured. In fact, creativity is based on something that virtually everyone is born with: imagination. People from widely diverse backgrounds and educational experiences have made creative, innovative contributions to all aspects of art, culture, science, and knowledge through the ages. And although youth can be an advantage in a few professions, like theoretical mathematics and sports, there is no age limit to creative work—Picasso was painting and sculpting some of his most inventive work in his seventies and eighties.

Creativity and innovation can be nurtured by learning environments that foster questioning, patience, openness to fresh ideas, high levels of trust, and learning from mistakes and failures. They can be developed, like many other skills, through practice over time. Though there is no accepted universal test for creativity and innovation skills, hundreds of instruments and assessment tools exist, each one measuring different aspects of creativity in a specific field, from math and music to writing and robotics.

Throughout the SARS project, the students on the team continually exercised their creativity and innovation skills: they invented a simulation game where users attempt to avert an outbreak of SARS in the fictional country of Asitwon, they designed creative animations that demonstrated the effects of the virus in action, and they came up with innovative ways to illustrate often complex medical concepts.

The SARS students were honing many of the component skills that lead to increased levels of creativity and innovation. Thinking creatively, closely related to thinking critically and solving problems, is at the core of creative work. Collaborating with others to further develop and refine creative ideas becomes applied creativity and leads to useful real-world innovations, a prize skill in our 21st century innovation-driven economy.

Numerous collections of learning exercises and activities have been designed to develop specific aspects of creativity and innovation. One popular example in playing card format is Roger von Oech's Creative Whack Pack of strategies to improve creativity.[8] Figure 3.3 shows two sample cards.

One of the most effective ways to develop creative skills is through design challenge projects in which students must invent solutions to real-world problems, such as designing a solar vest

Creativity and Innovation Skills

Students should be able to:

Think creatively

- Use a wide range of idea creation techniques (such as brainstorming)
- Create novel, new and worthwhile ideas (both incremental and radical concepts)
- Elaborate, refine, analyze and evaluate their own ideas in order to improve and maximize creative efforts

Work creatively with others

- Develop, implement and communicate new ideas to others effectively
- Be open and responsive to new and diverse perspectives; incorporate group input and feedback into the work
- Demonstrate originality and inventiveness in work and understand the real world limits to adopting new ideas
- View failure as an opportunity to learn; understand that creativity and innovation is a long-term, cyclical process of small successes and frequent mistakes

Implement innovations

- Act on creative ideas to make a tangible and useful contribution to the field in which the innovation will occur

Source: Copyright © Partnership for 21st Century Skills. Reprinted by permission of the Partnership for 21st Century Skills, www.21stcenturyskills.org.

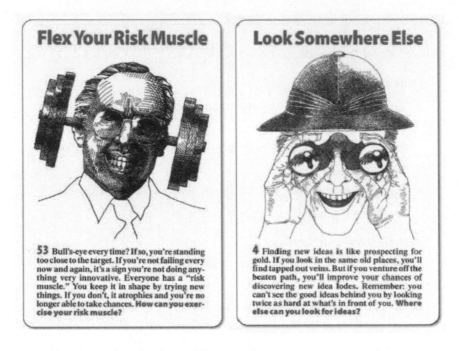

Flex Your Risk Muscle

53 Bull's-eye every time? If so, you're standing too close to the target. If you're not failing every now and again, it's a sign you're not doing anything very innovative. Everyone has a "risk muscle." You keep it in shape by trying new things. If you don't, it atrophies and you're no longer able to take chances. **How can you exercise your risk muscle?**

Look Somewhere Else

4 Finding new ideas is like prospecting for gold. If you look in the same old places, you'll find tapped out veins. But if you venture off the beaten path, you'll improve your chances of discovering new idea lodes. Remember: you can't see the good ideas behind you by looking twice as hard at what's in front of you. **Where else can you look for ideas?**

Figure 3.3.   Creative Whack Pack Creativity Cards.

that can charge a cell phone when worn in the sun. (We discuss design challenge projects further in Part Three.)

Critical thinking and problem solving, communication and collaboration, and creativity and innovation are three top-drawer skill sets in our toolbox for learning, work, and life in the 21st century. Powering these learning and innovation skills are the knowledge tools and technologies of our times. This leads us to the next three skills in the framework for learning's future: the information, media, and technology digital literacy skills discussed in the next chapter.

4

Digital Literacy Skills

INFO-SAVVY, MEDIA-FLUENT, TECH-TUNED

It is no longer enough simply to read and write. Students must also become literate in the understanding of visual images. Our children must learn how to spot a stereotype, isolate a social cliché, and distinguish facts from propaganda, analysis from banter, and important news from coverage.

—Ernest Boyer, past president, Carnegie Foundation
for the Advancement of Teaching

Before talking about the most obviously 21st century part of the P21 learning rainbow, the three digital literacy skills, take a moment to consider the sidebar, a fable about an unlucky kingdom that briefly blundered onto the bleeding edge of history.

Whether we're ready or not, the Knowledge Age has arrived, and today's World Wide Web version of King Wallace's World Wide Wall is fast becoming a permanent part of our everyday lives.

While we have not yet reached the good king's utopian dream of Learnalot, the Learning Society for all, we certainly have had our share of early experiences with the good, the bad, and the ugly sides of the wide-open communications and unrestricted online commerce and social networking projected in the fable.

The Once and Future Kingdom of Learning

In a kingdom long ago, but not too far away, there reigned an extraordinarily farsighted ruler, King Wallace, and his wonderfully practical and competent wife, Queen Nettie.

One stormy night, after a contentious day at court, King Wallace had an unusually vivid dream. He envisioned his kingdom transformed into a beauteously tranquil paradise dedicated to the glorious pursuit of learning, where all the world's knowledge was easily accessible all day every day, inscribed on a myriad of intricate stone walls throughout the land.

The kingdom was called Learnalot [trumpet fanfare].

In his dream, King Wallace gazed with amazement upon his loyal subjects, young and old, poring over the timeless words and great thoughts of the ages, chiseling brilliant new ideas, inventions, epic poems, and songs of great beauty and truth, all on this vast network of walls, hailed as the Great Wall of King Wallace.

The king watched as the Hard Ware Guild (the masons) furiously mortared stone upon stone to expand the network infrastructure, while the Soft Ware Guild (the plasterers) spread smooth, rewriteable firewall clay in countless even lines, forming neat rows and tables ready for users to inscribe, online, their data upon this base.

And this ever-increasing monument to technological innovation stretched far beyond the horizon, to the four corners of the firmament, until all the countless realms of the known world were connected to the one great World Wide Wall.

What moved him almost to tears, though, were the peaceful, contented faces of the people—so happy to dwell in a land where each and every soul could become learned and realize every inborn potential, where learning was truly king (next to His Royal Highness, that is).

"Ahhh," he thought in his dream, "if only *I* could rule over such a peaceable and noble Knowledge Society."

When he awoke, he found Queen Nettie gazing out the window with a most unbecoming look of horror. "Look my Lord," she gasped, "something awful has befallen our kingdom—there are walls strewn hither and yon like a frightful maze of dragons upon the land. I knew you shouldn't have insulted Morelan the Magician last night!"

"'Tis just like my dream," King Wallace muttered as he wobbled over to the window. "Yet a dream it surely is not—it is altogether real!"

"Oh, my beloved Queen," he exclaimed, dramatically sweeping his outstretched arm across the panoramic view from the turret window, "behold . . . Learnalot! [trumpet fanfare]—the Noble Kingdom of Learning. And we, my dearest, are the Laudatory Lord and Leading Lady of Learning, the Magnificent Monarchs of Immortal Memorabilia, the Paragons of Pedagogical Prodigiousness, the . . . "

"I smell trouble," interrupted Queen Nettie.

And down below in the streets, they witnessed an astonishing unfolding of walled-in sights: knights directing their pages to inscribe jousting tournament schedules, noting the odds and where bets could be made; the owner of the Upin Arms pub posting advertisements for a two-night, all-you-can-drink special; an entire section of the wall devoted to buying, selling, and auctioning everything imaginable, all under an enormous "Wall Mart" sign; an entire thoroughfare, "Wall Street," dedicated to betting on the future prices of barley, butter, and beer; and much worse: lurid illustrations that would bring a blush to the face of any righteous mortal of the realm, plus a hefty subscription fee to fully reveal more unholy images.

What a nasty nightmare!

Soon there grew an uprising and wall-to-wall demands for a wall hanging of the king, led by Sir Ludd (with music provided by his midi-evil minstrel band, the Luddites). Their political platform rested on "the protection of the young and innocent from Wall Spam, the riddance of Crass Commercialization from the Commons, and the Resurrection of Declining Moral and Common Sense Standards."

The protestors were soon joined by the Union of Serf Farmers, whose crops were blighted by the shade from "all them bloody walls."

Day and night thousands marched through the shadowed rat maze of walls, voices united in one unending chant, tight-clenched fists raised with each thundering cry: "Off the Wall! Off the Wall! Off the Wall!"

Then one morning, as if a billion dotted bombs burst without sound, the walls crumbled and vanished into thin air. And everything seemed more peaceful and beauteous than ever before.

King Wallace turned to his Queen. "Alas, my Lady, you were right all along. We are not in the least ready for the great Knowledge Age or the noble Learning Society.

"'Tis time to return to *your* plans my dearest—stronger fishnets for the fishermen, improved plows for the plowmen, better yeos for the yeomen—sensible solutions for our people and our times.

"Perhaps, my dear, one fine day in the far-off future, there will come a time when learning is truly king."

"And queen," added Her Highness.

All the more reason that our 21st century students need to acquire the skills to appropriately access, evaluate, use, manage, and add to the wealth of information and media they now have at their thumbs and fingertips.

With today's and tomorrow's digital tools, our net generation students will have unprecedented power to amplify their ability to think, learn, communicate, collaborate, and create. Along with all that power comes the need to learn the appropriate skills to handle massive amounts of information, media, and technology.

And so we return to the 21st century skill rainbow to consider:

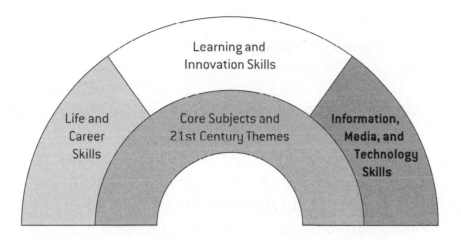

Figure 4.1.   The 21st Century Knowledge-and-Skills Rainbow.

- Information literacy
- Media literacy
- Information and communication technology (ICT) literacy

Information Literacy

In the 21st century, everyone's level of information literacy and fluency will need to rise. Whether at work, in school, at home, or in the community, there will be increasing demands on our ability to

- Access information efficiently and effectively
- Evaluate information critically and competently
- Use information accurately and creatively[1]

In the SARS project, a tremendous amount of medical, scientific, sociological, and governmental information had to be collected, reviewed, compared, analyzed, summarized, and visualized for the students' Web site.

The students had to make sure the information was credible, accurate, and reliable. They had to decide which information was most useful and interesting and how to organize and display it to keep their users—students like themselves—engaged.

They also had to analyze and deal with ethical issues: In a large-scale viral pandemic like SARS, were the decisions as to who should be informed first the right decisions? How should information about preventing further spread of the disease be communicated? Would their Web site help people understand the disease better, or could it cause more fear?

The SARS students were applying all the component skills of Information Literacy in the P21 framework.

Many online resources are available for building information literacy skills (see Appendix A). Some of the best are from the American Association of School Librarians (AASL), who believe that librarians are becoming 21st century "digital directors" championing the effective use of information technologies in schools (see Appendix A). Their numerous publications and information literacy guides clearly explain such lessons as the importance of primary as opposed to secondary resources in research and how to assess the credibility of online information using corroborating evidence from multiple reliable sources.

Accessing, evaluating, applying, and managing information well, and using information sources appropriately and effectively, are just some of the skills that define 21st century digital literacy. Understanding how different types of media are used

Information Literacy Skills

Students should be able to:

Access and evaluate information

- Access information efficiently (time) and effectively (sources)
- Evaluate information critically and competently

Use and manage information

- Use information accurately and creatively for the issue or problem at hand
- Manage the flow of information from a wide variety of sources
- Apply a fundamental understanding of the ethical/legal issues surrounding the access and use of information

Source: Copyright © Partnership for 21st Century Skills. Reprinted by permission of the Partnership for 21st Century Skills, www.21stcenturyskills.org.

to communicate messages, how to choose from the many media choices now available, and how to create effective messages in a variety of media are also important.

We turn to those media-oriented skills next.

Media Literacy

Surrounded by digital media and media choices, 21st century students need to understand how to best apply the media resources available for learning, and to use media creation tools to create compelling and effective communication products such as videos, audio podcasts, and Web sites.

According to the Center for Media Literacy, media literacy skills provide "a framework to access, analyze, evaluate and create messages in a variety of forms, build an understanding of the role of media in society, as well as [develop] the essential skills of inquiry and self-expression."[2]

"Media literacy" in this context refers to the medium of delivering messages (print, graphics, animation, audio, video, Web sites, and so on), the crafting of the message for a particular medium—the graphic "look and feel" of a Web site, for example, and the impacts the media message has on audiences. As the SARS team members demonstrated, it takes a high level of media literacy to select the right medium for a particular topic; obtain the proper permissions to reuse others' material; design and create Web pages, graphics, animations, videos, and games (including selecting the right digital tools for the tasks); and even choose the appropriate communication methods to promote their work to other students.

All these skills go into building media literacy.

Organizations such as the Center for Media Literacy offer a variety of learning resources on topics ranging from the impact of media on youth smoking habits to the influence of media stars on young people's values, from the history of visual communications to the camera and editing techniques used in documentary videos. (See Appendix A for further resources.)

ICT Literacy

Information and communication technologies, or ICTs, are the quintessential tools of the 21st century. As discussed in Chapter

Media Literacy Skills

Students should be able to:

Analyze media

- Understand both how and why media messages are constructed, and for what purposes
- Examine how individuals interpret messages differently, how values and points of view are included or excluded and how media can influence beliefs and behaviors
- Apply a fundamental understanding of the ethical and legal issues surrounding the access and use of media

Create media products

- Understand and utilize the most appropriate media creation tools, characteristics and conventions
- Understand and effectively utilize the most appropriate expressions and interpretations in diverse, multicultural environments

Source: Copyright © Partnership for 21st Century Skills. Reprinted by permission of the Partnership for 21st Century Skills, www.21stcenturyskills.org.

Two, the net generation, today's "digital natives," are "bathed in bits" from birth, clutching remote controls, computer mice, and cell phones from an early age.

But using these tools well for learning is another story. A number of international organizations have been at work for decades to help close the world's digital learning divides and provide guidance on how best to use the expanding toolbox of ICT power tools for learning.

International standards for the educational use of technology have been created for students, teachers, and administrators by the International Society for Technology in Education (ISTE) and UNESCO[3] and hundreds of organizations around the globe are dedicated to helping integrate ICTs into the daily work of schools and education systems.

Though our tech-tuned 21st century students are often more fluent in the use of technology than their parents or teachers, they will always need guidance in how to best apply these powerful tools to complex learning and creative tasks.

Assessing the risks of using personal images and commercial music on a social networking Web site such as Facebook or YouTube often requires critical thinking, sound judgment, and an understanding of potential future consequences—considerations where students can certainly benefit from some firm adult guidance.

As the SARS project students demonstrated, the hard work comes in applying ICT tools effectively to advance your own learning while creating communication products that help others learn about the issue you care about.

There are a wide range of ICT literacy resources from many international organizations such as ISTE and the Consortium for School Networking (CoSN), from national organizations such as Becta (formerly the British Educational Communications and Technology Agency), from numerous ICT hardware and software suppliers, and from a wide variety of learning technology and education organizations. (See Appendix A for further resources.)

The three digital literacy skills—information, media, and ICT literacy—are continually evolving, and they are all essential to

ICT Literacy Skills

Students should be able to:

Apply technology effectively

- Use technology as a tool to research, organize, evaluate and communicate information
- Use digital technologies (computers, PDAs, media players, GPS, etc.), communication/networking tools and social networks appropriately to access, manage, integrate, evaluate, and create information in order to successfully function in a knowledge economy
- Apply a fundamental understanding of the ethical/legal issues surrounding the access and use of information technologies

Source. Copyright © Partnership for 21st Century Skills. Reprinted by permission of the Partnership for 21st Century Skills, www.21stcenturyskills.org.

managing our ever-expanding tool sets of information, media, and communications technologies. These 21st century literacies are also powering the learning of many of the other skills in the P21 framework's rainbow.

In the next chapter we look at some of the age-old personal skills—the life and career skills—that are becoming more in demand as technology enhances learning, work, and life in the 21st century.

5

Career and Life Skills

WORK-READY, PREPARED FOR LIFE

Imagine that the SARS team Web site project was an actual project of a global company that publishes medical information for the general public on the Internet. Imagine also that the team's Web site, just like the student project, had won an industry award for excellence in communication on a timely medical topic.

How would the manager of someone on the team evaluate that member's work at the close of the project?

The manager might use a set of performance evaluation criteria, a common practice in most businesses today, that includes both work outcomes and skill ratings. The results might look something like Table 5.1.

Though the set of evaluation criteria used to rate employee performance in this example includes virtually all of the 21st century skills we've discussed so far, the last five criteria—the career and life skills of the P21 learning framework (highlighted in Figure 5.1) are some of the performance qualities most often reviewed on employee evaluations.

We turn to these work and life skills next.

Table 5.1.   Performance Evaluation Criteria.

Employee Performance Evaluation Worksheet		
Criterion	*Evaluation Question*	*Rating (1–4)*
Overall work quality	Was the project work of high quality, as well as being delivered on time and on budget?	4
Technical competence	Did the employee demonstrate a high level of technical and operational skills and competence?	3
Problem solving	Did the employee solve problems effectively and efficiently as they arose?	4
Creativity and innovation	Did the employee come up with creative and innovative solutions to problems?	4
Communications	Were the employee's internal and external project communications efficient and effective?	3
Teamwork	Did the employee collaborate well with other members of the team?	4
Flexibility and adaptability	Did the employee demonstrate the flexibility to adapt to new and unexpected project changes?	3
Initiative and self-direction	Did the employee show personal initiative, self-motivation, and self-directedness in all project work?	4
Social and cross-cultural skills	Did the employee exhibit strong social skills and cross-cultural understanding of diverse team members?	3
Productivity and accountability	Was the employee productive in use of time and other resources and in accounting for all project details?	3
Leadership and responsibility	Did the employee demonstrate leadership qualities and take responsibility for the success of the project work?	4
	Total	39
	Overall Rating	Exceeds Expectations

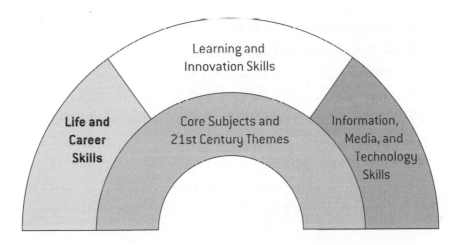

Figure 5.1. The 21st Century Knowledge-and-Skills Rainbow.

Flexibility and Adaptability

In times of change learners inherit the earth, while the
learned find themselves beautifully equipped to deal with
a world that no longer exists.
—Eric Hoffer

We are in a time of great change. Flexibility and adaptability are now essential skills for learning, work, and citizenship in the 21st century.

The rapid pace of technological change forces us all to adapt quickly to new ways of communicating, learning, working, and living. We switch jobs and careers more frequently, and entirely new kinds of work are arising from innovations in many fields.

One of the few unchanging aspects of the 21st century knowledge economy is the universal need to organize work into well-defined projects carried out by global project teams on tight time schedules with limited resources.

Whether the project at hand is for school, work, or around the home, we all know it can take an unexpected turn that requires rapid changes to our plans. Adjusting and adapting strategies to accommodate new circumstances is an essential "flex-ability" that everyone must develop in fast-changing times.

The ability to adapt—such as shifting to a whole new way of looking at the problem at hand—can turn the unexpected to your advantage, resulting in uniquely creative solutions and true innovations that can help meet the 21st century demand for fresh ideas and approaches.

The SARS Project team faced a number of tough challenges, both technically, in implementing their Web site design, and collaboratively, in trying to coordinate their work across the globe. Some of the best features of their Web site came from unexpected solutions to their technical problems. For example, as the deadline for the competition approached, team members were able to use their different time zones to their advantage—passing text written in one time zone to the graphics artist in the next for illustration, then on to the programmer in the third zone to assemble all the elements into a working Web page, and finally to the project coordinator to test, edit, and suggest revisions for the team's next round of work. This allowed project work to continue around the clock.

As the employee performance evaluation form in Table 4.1 suggests, another type of flexibility and adaptability that is valuable today is the ability to deal with criticism, setbacks, and even failure.

The skills involved in flexibility and adaptability can be learned by working on progressively more complex projects that challenge

Flexibility and Adaptability Skills

Students should be able to:

Adapt to change

- Adapt to varied roles, job responsibilities, schedules, and contexts
- Work effectively in a climate of ambiguity and changing priorities

Be flexible

- Incorporate feedback effectively
- Deal positively with praise, setbacks and criticism
- Understand, negotiate and balance diverse views and beliefs to reach workable solutions, particularly in multi-cultural environments

Source: Copyright © Partnership for 21st Century Skills. Reprinted by permission of the Partnership for 21st Century Skills, www.21stcenturyskills.org.

student teams to change course when things aren't working well, adapt to new developments in the project, and incorporate new team members on both current and new projects. Students can also develop high degrees of flexibility and adaptability as part of a "tech support" team for their school, helping their teachers to quickly solve technology problems as they arise. (See Appendix A for further resources.)

Initiative and Self-Direction

The best place to find a helping hand is at the end of your own arm.
—Old Swedish Proverb

In our always-on, fast-paced, flattened world of work, time for extended training and motivational development is in very short supply. Workers must arrive motivated, ready to use their initiative to get things done, and prepared to be highly self-reliant in everyday work.

The amount of time busy managers have for mentoring and guiding employees is quickly diminishing. Time, goals, project plans, workload, and "just-in-time" learning must all be self-managed and self-directed in today's wound-up work world.

Though teachers may be familiar with having a fairly high level of independence and autonomy in their classrooms, helping students become more self-reliant and independent as learners has always been a challenge. Technology is helping, though, providing a wealth of always-on self-service tools for researching and learning online.

The teacher coaches of the SARS team were amazed at the level of self-direction, motivation, and independence their students demonstrated. They asked for help at the start of the project, especially technical help in selecting and using the right tools to create their Web site, and occasionally during the course of the project when they hit particularly tricky technical issues. Otherwise, they mostly relied on each other to help solve problems or to find answers to their questions on the Internet. As one of the coaches said, "The best thing about this group is, they know what they want and they just go for it."

Today's students must prepare for the reality of 21st century work and develop deeper levels of initiative and self-direction skills as they progress through school. Offering each student the appropriate level of freedom to exercise self-direction and initiative is an ongoing, universal challenge for both teachers and parents. Music, dance, and theater performances; mentorships, apprenticeships, internships, and community service projects; and student-developed projects and hobbies all provide good opportunities to develop a passion for a subject and to exercise self-motivation, initiative, and self-direction.

Initiative and Self-Direction Skills

Students should be able to:

Manage goals and time

- Set goals with tangible and intangible success criteria
- Balance tactical (short-term) and strategic (long-term) goals
- Utilize time and manage workload efficiently

Work independently

- Monitor, define, prioritize and complete tasks without direct oversight

Be self-directed learners

- Go beyond basic mastery of skills and/or curriculum to explore and expand one's own learning and opportunities to gain expertise
- Demonstrate initiative to advance skill levels toward a professional level
- Demonstrate commitment to learning as a lifelong process
- Reflect critically on past experiences in order to inform future progress

Source: Copyright © Partnership for 21st Century Skills. Reprinted by permission of the Partnership for 21st Century Skills, www.21stcenturyskills.org.

Social and Cross-Cultural Interaction

Diversity is the one thing we all have in common.
—Anonymous

Diverse work teams, scattered around the globe and connected by technology, are becoming the norm for 21st century work. Diverse schools and communities are also becoming more common worldwide.

The ability to work effectively and creatively with team members and classmates regardless of differences in culture and style is an essential 21st century life skill. Understanding and accommodating cultural and social differences, and using these differences to come up with even more creative ideas and solutions to problems, will be increasingly important throughout our century.

Recent research on the importance of emotional and social intelligence to a child's development and to successful learning has led to a wide variety of programs and learning materials that support social skills and social responsibility.[1] One excellent example is the classroom learning materials on building more connected and respectful environments for learning available from Educators for Social Responsibility (ESR). From practical and constructive methods for resolving conflict between students to procedures for creating a team contract before working together on a collaborative project, ESR offers a wide range of well-tested learning activities and methods for creating more pro-social learning environments (see Appendix A for further resources).

Students are successfully developing cross-cultural interaction skills both online and face-to-face, as the international team in the SARS project did. A number of organizations have created excellent materials to further develop students' cross-cultural understanding—a notable example is the Asia Society, whose excellent reports and curriculum resources are helping teachers and students go global in their learning. The cross-sharing of firsthand reports of what daily life is like for students in other countries and a wide variety of cross-cultural student exchanges and projects that the Asia Society and others sponsor are giving students a better sense of how we are all different and all the same.

The skills to become socially adept, cross-culturally fluent global learners and citizens are more important than ever.

Social and Cross-Cultural Skills

Students should be able to:

Interact effectively with others

- Know when it's appropriate to listen and when to speak
- Conduct themselves in a respectable, professional manner

Work effectively in diverse teams

- Respect cultural differences and work effectively with people from a range of social and cultural backgrounds
- Respond open-mindedly to different ideas and values
- Leverage social and cultural differences to create new ideas and increase innovation and quality of work

Source: Copyright © Partnership for 21st Century Skills. Reprinted by permission of the Partnership for 21st Century Skills, www.21stcenturyskills.org.

Productivity and Accountability

Efficiency is doing things right; effectiveness is doing the
right things.
—Peter Drucker

Productive workers and learners have been in demand in both
business and education down the centuries. Setting and meeting
goals, prioritizing work, and using time well are all skills that support working and learning equally well.

With an expanding toolkit of knowledge work tools designed
to boost personal and group productivity, both efficiency and
effectiveness in learning and work are increasing dramatically.
Technology is also easing the burden of accountability—the tracking and sharing of work done and lessons learned.

Projects—defining, planning, executing, and evaluating
them—have become the currency of 21st century work. And
learning projects are also becoming more important as a unit of
instruction in 21st century learning. Good project management
skills are crucial to both work and learning projects, and a number of programs are helping teachers and students better manage the "learning project cycle." (More on what this project cycle
contains and how it can be applied to learning projects can be
found in Chapter Seven.) Professional development programs for
teachers wanting to develop effective learning projects for their
students are offered by a number of organizations including
the Oracle Education Foundation (see the Project Learning
Institute video segment on the DVD included in this book,
on this book's Web site at http://21stcenturyskillsbook.com,

or at the OEF Web site, http://oraclefoundation.org/single_player
.html?v=5), Intel's Teach program, the Buck Institute of Education,
the Project Management Institute Education Foundation, The
Coalition of Essential Schools, and others (see Appendix A for
further information).

Productivity and accountability are important skill sets that
all 21st century students and teachers need for success in school,
work, and life.

Productivity and Accountability Skills

Students should be able to:

Manage projects
- Set and meet goals, even in the face of obstacles and competing pressures
- Prioritize, plan and manage work to achieve the intended result

Produce results
- Demonstrate additional attributes associated with producing high-quality products including:
  - Work positively and ethically
  - Manage time and projects effectively
  - Multitask
  - Participate actively, as well as be reliable and punctual
  - Present oneself professionally and with proper etiquette
  - Collaborate and cooperate effectively with teams
  - Respect and appreciate team diversity
  - Be accountable for results

Source: Copyright © Partnership for 21st Century Skills. Reprinted by permission of the Partnership for 21st Century Skills, www.21stcenturyskills.org.

Leadership and Responsibility

Change will not come if we wait for some other person or
some other time. We are the ones we've been waiting for.
We are the change that we seek.
—President Barack Obama

The SARS team demonstrated the kind of leadership skills that
will be needed more and more in the 21st century—distributed
leadership and responsibility.

Though the SARS team had an overall team coordinator—
Van from Philadelphia—each team member was responsible for
a part of the work that needed to be done, but each also had to
be mindful of how that part would be woven into other work
done by other team members. Three levels of responsibility and
teamwork—individual leadership, coordination between team
members, and overall team collaboration toward a common
vision—were important to the success of the SARS project.

People coming together to work on a project they care about,
dividing the work up among the team, taking on roles that play to
their strengths, everyone contributing to a creative outcome and
celebrating the results, then each person moving on to the next
project with a different set of players, has been called the "studio
model"—for the ways that films and television programs are produced in media production studios.

This project-based, studio model of work is becoming more
prevalent in the knowledge work economy, and will be an important work style to master in the 21st century.

The studio model also offers students a powerful style of learning that can provide lots of opportunities to take responsibility and exercise leadership—skills important to future employers. The studio project model of learning can also help build many of the other 21st century skills in the P21 framework, such as collaboration, communications, and cross-cultural understanding.

A wide number of student leadership programs already focus on developing these skills, from local, national, and international perspectives. One example of an international leadership development program is the Model UN program, where students simulate a United Nations meeting to deal with a particular international crisis, with each student delegate representing the views of a particular country (see Appendix A for further examples).

Leadership and Responsibility Skills

Students should be able to:

Guide and lead others
- Use interpersonal and problem-solving skills to influence and guide others toward a goal
- Leverage strengths of others to accomplish a common goal
- Inspire others to reach their very best via example and selflessness
- Demonstrate integrity and ethical behavior in using influence and power

Be responsible to others
- Act responsibly with the interests of the larger community in mind

Source: Copyright © Partnership for 21st Century Skills. Reprinted by permission of the Partnership for 21st Century Skills, www.21stcenturyskills.org.

The life and career skills detailed in this chapter are essential to both work and learning in the 21st century. Though these skills have been around for a very long time, they take on new significance with the digital power tools now available for work and learning. They will no doubt be important skills to have right into the 22nd century.

As we look back over all eleven of the 21st century skills detailed in Chapters Three, Four, and Five, an important question arises: How are we ever going to make sure that all students have an opportunity to learn these skills along with the core subjects and contemporary themes needed for a well-rounded 21st century education?

Answers to this question will be explored next in Part Three.

PART THREE

21ST CENTURY LEARNING IN PRACTICE

6

21st Century Learning and Teaching

The power to question is the basis of all human progress.
—Indira Ghandi

Our problems are man-made, therefore they may be solved by man. No problem of human destiny is beyond human beings.
—John F. Kennedy

Question: What are the important tools we need to support a 21st century approach to learning and teaching?

a. The Internet
b. Pen and paper
c. Cell phones
d. Educational games
e. Tests and quizzes
f. A good teacher
g. Educational funding
h. Loving parents
i. All of the above

Answer: All of the above. But two important things are missing.

All of these items contribute to a 21st century education, but two key tools not on this list may be the most powerful learning tools ever devised:

- *Questions* and the process to uncover their answers
- *Problems* and the inventing of their possible solutions

Learning the P's and Q's: Problems and Questions

The learning power of the right question at the right time has been celebrated throughout recorded history. Philosophers, education theorists, and thought leaders from Confucius to Socrates and Plato to John Dewey, Jerome Bruner, Seymour Papert, and others have placed questioning and inquiry at the heart of learning and understanding.

The careful construction of basic questions about our natural world and the imaginative search for accurate answers to them are at the center of the scientific method—our most important innovation for exploring and uncovering new knowledge. For instance, Einstein's early wondering about what it would be like to travel on a light beam initiated a lifelong search for understanding and led to the greatest discoveries in 20th century physics.

Learning through solving problems goes back much further in time, to the first humans to plant seeds and domesticate animals, ensuring a local supply of food and the beginnings of agriculture. Problems have been the perennial motivators for tool making, invention, religion, laws, science, engineering, business, and the evolution of virtually all our modern technologies and societal institutions.

Thomas Edison's celebrated year-and-a-half search for the right materials to make an effective incandescent electric light bulb (plus the wiring, sockets, fuses, and generators to go with it) eventually improved the quality of life for most people—although well over a billion people still live without electricity in the 21st century.[1] His passionate and tireless persistence in solving perplexing problems has been the archetype for engineers, technologists, and learners ever since.

Roads to Answers and Solutions: Science and Engineering

Questions and problems are the foundations for the two most powerful approaches humankind has yet developed for gaining new knowledge and creating new ways of living: science and engineering. Figure 6.1 illustrates the central role questions and problems play in science and in engineering and technology:[2]

Scientists approach the world with questions: *Why is the sky blue? What is the smallest particle in the universe? What causes cancer? How does burning fossil fuels affect the climate?* They then use a rigorous method to discover and verify answers to their questions—the *scientific experimental method.*

Engineers and inventors on the other hand are motivated by challenging problems: *How can I make this airplane safer? How can we store more data in a smaller space? How can we use the sun's energy to heat and power our homes?* Engineers use a slightly different method to design, build, and test solutions to their problems: the *engineering design method.*

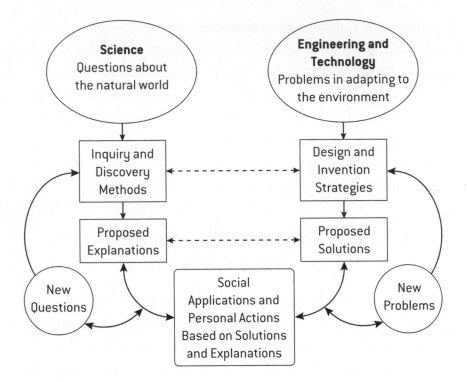

Figure 6.1.   Science and Technology, Questions and Problems.

Though these methods are similar, they differ in the way answers and solutions are devised and tested, as shown in Table 6.1.

Scientists use experiments to test an explanation or hypothesis, and engineers devise prototypes or create new designs to see how well their solution works. Applying both scientific and engineering methods to basic questions and the problems of our times has vastly accelerated the growth of new knowledge, new skills, and the innovations of modern living. Along with the arts and culture, and our evolving social and political structures, science and engineering have propelled human progress.

Table 6.1.   Scientific Versus Engineering Methods.

Scientific Experimental Method	Engineering Design Method
Pose a question	Define a problem
Research the question	Research the problem
Construct an answer, explanation, or hypothesis to be tested	Design, plan, and build a prototype or solution to be tested
Test the hypothesis through experiments that attempt to disprove it	Test the prototype or solution to see if it solves the problem
Analyze the results and draw a conclusion about the answer	Analyze the results and improve the solution to the problem
Communicate the results and compare with others' results	Communicate the results and implement or market the solution as a product or service
Repeat the process with more refined questions or with new questions that arose in the process	Repeat the process with refined or new ideas for better solutions, or with new problems that arose in the process

Questions and problems are also the natural motivators for learning: Why? is a favorite question of curious young children, and persistence in asking why? well into adulthood can lead to deeper insights and to further questions that inspire lifelong searches for answers to mysteries still unsolved. Puzzling problems that demand fresh ideas in the pursuit of new and better solutions can lead to creative, even breakthrough results and have been the source of useful inventions and innovations great and small throughout history.

The journeys to discover answers to *why?* and to creating innovative solutions to our perplexing *how-can-we . . . ?* problems are authentic learning adventures—they deepen understanding, hone skills, provide emotional satisfaction (as well as some creative frustration), and reveal new ways to work, learn, and thrive in our world.

Teachers and parents have long known that asking open-ended questions and posing intriguing problems engage children's imaginations and help motivate them to explore, discover, create, and learn.

The learning method based on the power of questions is called *inquiry-based learning,* or just *inquiry,* and the method that uses the power of designing solutions to problems is called *design-based learning,* or just *design.*

Inquiry and design learning methods have been proven to be highly effective in engaging and sustaining learning and deepening understanding, as we discuss in the next chapter. These learning methods, combined with traditional ways of acquiring content knowledge and basic skills—guided by caring teachers and parents and powered by today's digital learning tools—are at the center of a 21st century approach to learning.

What would a 21st century learning model look like that uses the power of problems and questions—the "Ps and Qs" of engaged learning—to drive deep interest, understanding, caring, and the application of 21st century skills to real-world challenges? One such learning model, based on a human-powered vehicle familiar to all of us, is helping to transport more and more learners and teachers around the globe into the 21st century. We take this learning model for a test drive next.

7

Powerful Learning

PROVEN PRACTICES, RESEARCHED RESULTS

Learning is a lifelong journey, and on most journeys it is important to have a destination in mind and a reliable means of transport to get there. The next sidebar provides one example of a classroom on the road to 21st century learning.

During the course of this classroom project, many of the features of a 21st century learning balance outlined earlier in this book were demonstrated—rigorous science content learned through a hands-on, collaborative project approach; a real-world problem and challenge that motivated individual and team learning; both a student-centered and teacher-guided approach to learning; and others.

A video of the class's science project, Bacterial Transformation Lab, is included on the DVD accompanying this book; you can also view it on the book's Web site. Both the DVD and Web site also include reflections from teacher Annie Chien on the project learning method.

In the Laboratory of the School of the Future

The diverse students in Annie Chien's tenth-grade biology class were lucky to be in a school committed to helping them become proficient problem solvers, questioners, and lifelong learners. They were all members of an evolving 21st century learning community—the School of the Future in New York City.

Annie's students were studying how genes work and how they can be altered for medical benefit, or "gene therapy," in the emerging bioengineering field. Their challenge was to physically transfer the genes that make one kind of bacteria glow under fluorescent light to another kind of bacteria that did not have this trait. By transferring these genes the students would also transfer the glowing bacteria's genetic capacity to resist a certain antibiotic to other bacteria that were not yet resistant to this antibiotic. [This is a common high school biology experiment that is entirely safe, using bacteria and procedures that present no risk to the students.]

In the process of preparing and conducting the experiment, the students had to clearly communicate their questions, research and find answers, learn from each other's findings, collaborate in teams to design and perform an experiment, solve problems, write up their results, present their findings, and manage their learning—all important 21st century skills.

The 21st Century Project Learning Bicycle

Let's look at how the learning approach used in Annie Chien's classroom works in terms of a learning model that can meet the needs of 21st century learners and the demands of our times—a model learning vehicle designed to transport students toward the goal of becoming more successful 21st century learners, workers, and citizens.

This model—the Project Learning Bicycle—provides a visual device to help remember the components of a well-designed and well-managed learning project. We have presented this model to educators around the world, and it always brings a smile as well as a welcome dose of insight into just what is meant by effective 21st century learning methods.

The Wheels—Define, Plan, Do, Review

The core of the learning model is the project itself. All projects, from baking a cake to building a house, have stages or phases that occur in a sequence, though backtracking and jumping around among the phases often occurs. The Project Learning Bicycle model has four project phases:

- Define
- Plan
- Do
- Review

The project must first be *defined*, with the question, problem, issue, or challenge that drives the learning in the project stated clearly and concisely. In the Bacteria Lab, the essential question was "How can we alter an organism's genes for medical use?" or as one student succinctly described the challenge, "How can we transfer glowing to another bacteria that can't?"

Teacher Annie Chien had a lot of *planning* to do for this project up front. She had to collect and prepare all the lab equipment for the experiment, set up the procedures for the student teams to follow, prepare the worksheets and lab recipe guides, and much more. The students also had to plan their individual and group work and the steps they would take to successfully carry out the experiment.

For a teacher to be an effective learning coach during a project (and not just a lecturer), learning activities must be designed so that the students own much of the learning and teaching. Students' planning their work, doing research, sharing findings with other team members, asking questions, designing procedures, taking on leadership and group facilitation roles, analyzing their own results, getting feedback from others, and so on are all important parts of a good project design that builds 21st century skills and deepens understanding of the learning content.

The extra time Annie Chien invested in planning student-directed activities paid off later on during the project, allowing her to give more individual attention and support to each learning team and its learning challenges.

After planning comes *doing:* the real work of the project must be accomplished, the learning activities performed, and the results recorded. Teacher and students work together, with the teacher playing the "conductor" or coach role, and the students being the team members or "workers" in the project.

Finally, the project results and lessons learned are presented and *reviewed.* The teacher, other students, and often other members of the learning community see the results in a presentation, exhibition, or learning fair and offer evaluations and feedback.

Lessons learned from going through the entire project cycle can often be applied to the next project, or sometimes to a new iteration of the same project, with the second time refining the project definition, improving the plan, refining project implementation, and resulting in deeper reflections and reviews. This way, learning grows and deepens.

Define, Plan, Do, and *Review*—these are the stages in the project learning and teaching cycles—the project "wheels"—for both the students and the teacher, as shown in Figure 7.1.

Though the time spent in each of the phases of a project may differ for the teacher and the student—the teacher typically spending more time in up-front planning and the students spending more time in the doing phase of project activities—both teacher and students work together through the project phases.

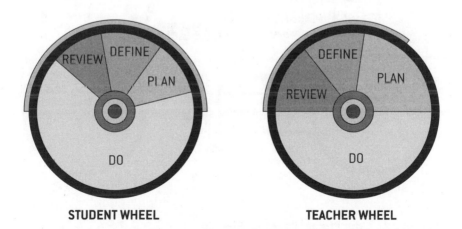

STUDENT WHEEL   **TEACHER WHEEL**

Figure 7.1.   Student and Teacher Project Wheels.

The Project Bicycle Frame and Components

With the project's wheels in place, we need a frame to hold the wheels together and to support the coordinated work of the project team. And to complete our two-wheeled learning vehicle, we need the other essential components—seats, handlebars, gears, pedals, brakes, and an additional electronic cyclometer to monitor speed, mileage, and time, and to record the trip's progress.

Students and teachers must coordinate their project cycle work, co-managing the whole learning project (the bicycle frame), and using the driving question or problem (the handlebars) to steer and guide the project forward, as in Figure 7.2.

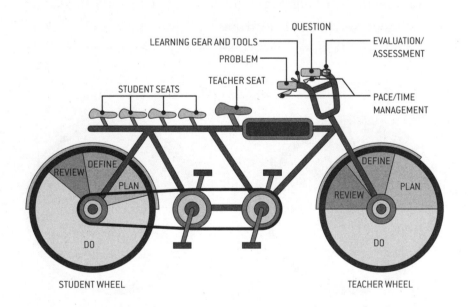

Figure 7.2.   The Project Learning Bicycle.

The learning gear used in the project (the lab equipment, Internet access for research, and all the rest) is represented by the gearshift, the gears, chain, derailleur, and so on; ongoing assessments of student learning (worksheets, questioning, observations, and lab reports) are represented by the cyclometer; and the pace and timing of the project is controlled by the bike's pedals and hand brakes.

On the Project Road

Once the project is launched ("on the road") the slope of the road represents the degree of challenge the project presents for the team—steep uphill climbs being more challenging than flat surfaces.

Balance is also important: if the project bicycle leans too far to the left, the teacher may be oversteering (applying too much direct instruction and control); too far to the right, and there may be too much collaborative creativity and independent construction of knowledge (referred to as "chaos" by one of the students in the Bacteria Lab video) without enough teacher guidance to ensure the desired learning objectives are achieved and the principles involved are understood. School and community support for this type of learning can provide a tailwind to help propel the project; lack of such support could be seen as strong headwinds to thwart progress. And finally, the goal is a rich learning experience that blends knowledge, understanding, and solid performance on many of the 21st century skills, as illustrated in Figure 7.3.

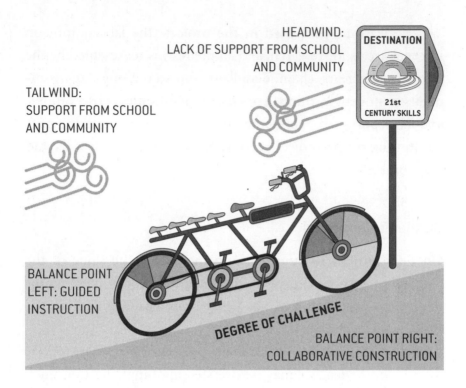

HEADWIND:
LACK OF SUPPORT FROM SCHOOL
AND COMMUNITY

DESTINATION

21st
CENTURY SKILLS

TAILWIND:
SUPPORT FROM SCHOOL
AND COMMUNITY

BALANCE POINT
LEFT: GUIDED
INSTRUCTION

DEGREE OF CHALLENGE

BALANCE POINT RIGHT:
COLLABORATIVE CONSTRUCTION

Figure 7.3.   The 21st Century Project Learning Bicycle Model.

A Successful Ride

The Bacteria Lab project closely followed the Bicycle model. The project was well defined, the students had their project phases to manage, the teacher had hers, and they co-managed the running of all the phases of the project fairly smoothly. The teacher played the learning coach role, stepping in for direct instruction when needed, and the students did most of the mental work of the project—researching, planning, analyzing, collaborating, experimenting, evaluating, and communicating.

Students had access to the necessary learning gear—lab equipment, bacteria cultures, clean room equipment, and computers for research. The pace of the project was appropriate (except for the actual experiment day, which was rather rushed), and the degree of challenge of the project was fitting for most of the students. A good balance was struck between direct instruction by the teacher and collaborative discovery and exploratory learning by the students throughout the project. Students gained a deeper understanding of science content through the hands-on engagement and questioning that naturally arose during their researching and experimenting.

The project had students exercising many of the 21st century skills—problem solving, communication, collaboration, information and ICT literacy, flexibility and adaptability, self-direction, leadership, and responsibility. The project did not particularly emphasize individual creativity and innovation, but the bioengineering expertise students gained did give them some insight into how scientists and engineers are innovating new approaches to medicine and gene therapy.

Designing and managing effective 21st century learning projects like the Bacteria Lab project is no small challenge—it has to engage and motivate diverse students, meet the curriculum goals of the school, provide evidence that each student is gaining understanding and proficiency, and prepare students for success in the real world with 21st century skills. This is especially a challenge for teachers who may have not been trained to teach in this way.

But as projects like the Bacteria Lab and the SARS Project described earlier illustrate, and as research and reports of successful learning projects from around the world reaffirm, this type of learning is very powerful. It deeply engages students in their learning, goes beyond memorization to meaningful understanding, and results in large learning gains for students with a wide range of learning styles and backgrounds.

Creativity Through Projects

Imagination is more important than knowledge.
—Albert Einstein

As we journey deeper into the 21st century, creativity and innovation will become the brightest stars in the constellation of 21st century skills. New ideas, innovative products, novel services, and fresh solutions to local and global problems will increasingly power our emerging Innovation Age.

Though there will be an increased demand for skills in science, technology, engineering, and math, the "STEM" skills, there will be even higher demands for creativity, invention, and innovation. The arts have been the traditional source for developing creativity. Integrating the arts into STEM (making it STEAM—an acronym whose first use is attributed to children's book author Peter Reynolds) will be an important education goal as we move through our century.

So how do we best prepare our students for a future of work that does not yet exist, careers that have not yet been invented, an economy that prizes things not yet created, and that puts STEAM into the learning plans for every child?

Tom Kelley, CEO of the renowned design firm IDEO has a one-word answer to this challenge— "design."[1] He is also a fan of a simple phrase that has launched a thousand design projects, "How might we . . . ?"

To prepare for the Age of Innovation we must all become better designers, ready to tackle brand-new problems and design things and processes that have never existed before.[2] We must apply both thinking and tinkering.

Fortunately the design process is not a secret ritual performed by a priestly cult of sanctified professionals. Everyone can participate in the design process, and as with playing a musical instrument or participating in a team sport, practice improves performance.

Learning projects anchored in the phases of the project cycle— define, plan, do, and review—can deeply engage students in their learning activities and build creative skills. Design challenges, like the ThinkQuest Web site competition and the FIRST Robotics contests, can go a long way in developing a student's invention and innovation skills.

IDEO has designed better toothbrushes, shopping carts, computer mice, e-commerce businesses, medical emergency room procedures, and thousands of other useful solutions to everyday challenges. The firm's design process follows the same four-phase project cycle, but with some important additions that boost the odds of a design team's coming up with innovative ideas and solutions:

- *Define.* Focus on a real-world problem or process whose solution will make things easier, better, faster, less expensive, more effective, or more enjoyable. The how-might-we question followed by the definition of the problem (for example, How might we use the sun's energy to inexpensively provide a nighttime flashlight for use in homes in rural areas without electricity?) is key to getting a design project off to a good start.

- *Plan.* Take the time to *understand* the users, clients, technology, market or field, and constraints on the problem. Closely and frequently *observe* how real people in real-life situations deal with the problem or condition at hand and create detailed profiles of typical people and their experiences with the issue.

A diverse design team is also important to the innovation process—the more diversity, the better the chance of coming up with a fresh, outside-the-box solution. (For example, the cultural diversity of the SARS Project team contributed to a number of Web site design innovations that appealed to a more international audience.)

- *Do.* Using a wide variety of visualizing and brainstorming techniques, come up with a wealth of possible design solutions and sort through the positives and negatives of each one. Choose the most promising design and create a prototype of it. Test it with a variety of real people in real problem situations and keep careful records of the results.
- *Review.* Evaluate and refine a series of prototypes in quick iterations, each time eliminating difficulties or confusion, enhancing the benefits, making better design trade-offs and improving the overall solution.

The *Do* and *Review* phases are repeated often in this stage of the IDEO cycle, bouncing back and forth between the two, with lessons learned from the evaluation immediately applied to the next round of creating an improved prototype.

Finally, the innovation is implemented, with client feedback and new ideas eventually prompting a brand-new trip through the design cycle and another quest for useful innovations.

IDEO's design process can be seen as a powerful project approach to learning. In fact the design process is a powerful learning process that produces innovative results, applies and builds the design team's creative skills, and develops a deep understanding of the problem area and its possible solutions.

Learning to design and designing to learn—the use of innovation-producing methods like the IDEO process will prepare students for the demands of the Innovation Age.

Evidence That Project Learning Works

Research evidence has proven that learning methods like those applied in the Bacteria Lab and the SARS Project and in learning frameworks like the Bicycle project learning model are successful at building deeper understanding and higher levels of motivation and engagement, and at developing the 21st century skills most needed for our times. What does the growing body of research say about the effectiveness of inquiry, design, and collaborative project approaches to learning?

- Students learn more deeply when they can apply classroom-gathered knowledge to real-world problems, and when they take part in projects that require sustained engagement and collaboration.

- Active and collaborative learning practices have a more significant impact on student performance than any other variable, including student background and prior achievement.
- Students are most successful when they are taught *how* to learn as well as *what* to learn.[3]

These summary conclusions are based on a thorough review of the fifty-year research base on inquiry, design, and collaborative approaches to learning by noted Stanford University education researcher, professor, and policy adviser Linda Darling-Hammond and her colleagues in *Powerful Learning—What We Know About Teaching for Understanding.*[4]

Professor Darling-Hammond and her colleagues reviewed the accumulated research on three learning approaches based on inquiry and design methods of teaching and learning: project learning, problem-based learning, and design-based learning. They also reviewed the extensive research literature on cooperative and small-group learning methods.

The following are the summary findings from their analyses of the research base for each of these learning methods, as well as highlights of key research studies for each method.

Collaborative Small-Group Learning

Students working in small teams on collective tasks have been the subject of hundreds of studies. All the research arrives at the same conclusion—there are significant benefits for students who work together on learning activities compared to students who work alone. The benefits include both greater individual and collective knowledge growth, better confidence and motivation levels, and improved social interactions and feelings toward other students.

In a comparison of four types of problems presented to both individuals and cooperative teams, researchers found that teams outperform individuals on all problem types and across all ages.[5] In addition, individuals who work in groups do better on individual assessments as well.[6]

Project Learning Methods

As illustrated by the SARS Project and the Bacteria Lab, project learning involves completing complex tasks that result in a realistic product, event, or presentation to an audience.[7]

Effective project learning has five key characteristics:[8]

- Project outcomes are tied to curriculum and learning goals.
- Driving questions and problems lead students to the central concepts or principles of the topic or subject area.
- Student investigations and research involve inquiry and knowledge building.
- Students are responsible for designing and managing much of their own learning.
- Projects are based on authentic, real-world problems and questions that students care about.

Research on learning projects having these qualities found that student gains in factual learning were equal to or better than those using more traditional classroom instructional methods. But when studies took the time to measure gains on other learning skills, in particular the higher-order, 21st century skills, the learning gains were significantly higher than traditional methods:

- A number of studies of whole-school models of project learning such as Expeditionary Learning[9] and Co-nect schools[10] show substantial gains in traditional test scores over comparison schools using more traditional methods. Whole-school models involve all the classrooms, teachers, students, and administrators in the project approach, not just a few innovating teachers in a few classrooms.
- In a study of fourth and fifth graders doing a project on housing shortages in different countries, project-learning students scored way above their traditional-learning control group on a critical-thinking test and in their learning confidence levels.[11]
- An ambitious three-year longitudinal study of students in two schools in England, matched for similar income and student achievement levels, found that significantly more students passed the National Exams in the school that used project approaches to learning math than in the school that used more traditional textbook and worksheet approaches. Project-learning students also developed more flexible and useful math knowledge than their textbook-oriented counterparts.[12]
- A study of the Challenge 2000 Multimedia Project in California showed that students in a project that created

multimedia brochures on the problems of homeless students scored much higher than a comparison group using more traditional methods in such areas as content mastery, audience sensitivity, and communication design.[13]

Other comparative studies documented a variety of benefits from project learning methods: increased ability to define problems, improved reasoning using clear arguments, and better planning of complex projects. Improvements in motivation, attitudes toward learning, and work habits were also found.

Another important research finding was that students who struggle with traditional textbook-and-lecture approaches benefited from a project learning approach that was better matched to their learning styles or preferences for working in groups.

Problem-Based Learning

A type of project learning, problem-based learning involves projects focused on solving complex, real-world problems using a case study approach. Students work in small groups to investigate, research, and create solutions to problems that could have multiple solutions and methods for reaching them.

Much of the research comes from medical education, where medical students are challenged to provide the proper diagnosis, tests, and treatment for a patient's case (based on real patient histories). This case method has also been used effectively in law and business education, as well as other professional learning, including teacher education.

Studies and meta-studies of the problem-based learning research show that, similar to the findings from project learning research, for factual learning, problem-based methods are equal to or better than traditional instruction. But problem-based methods far outshine traditional methods in developing 21st century skills like flexible problem solving and applying knowledge to real-world situations, as well as critical thinking skills such as generating testable hypotheses and communicating more coherent explanations.

The Cognition and Technology Group at Vanderbilt University (CTGV) studied problem approaches to learning for over a decade. In one study of more than seven hundred students from eleven school districts engaged in solving problems from CTGV's popular *Jasper Woodbury* series of video-based challenges, students experienced much larger gains than those in the comparison group for all five of the areas measured: understanding math concepts, doing word problems, planning approaches to problem solving, having positive attitudes toward math, and providing feedback to teachers.[14]

Design-Based Learning

Design-based learning approaches can be found across many subject disciplines including science, art, technology, engineering, and architecture. The SARS ThinkQuest Web site competition entry described earlier in this book is a classic example of a design-based challenge with a team of students collaboratively designing an educational Web site on a topic they care about.

- The international FIRST Robotics competition (www.usfirst .org) is another example of design-oriented learning where student teams design, build, and guide their robots in a competitive series of sports-like physical challenges.
- Learning through design is particularly popular in science education, where curriculum programs like Science by Design developed at the University of Michigan have high school students designing and building boats, greenhouses, and catapults.
- The Learning By Design curriculum developed by the Georgia Institute of Technology includes a wide range of design challenges that build understanding of essential scientific principles. In one of the Learning By Design studies, sixth-grade students designed and built a set of artificial lungs and working models of parts of the respiratory system. The study found that the learning-by-design students viewed the respiratory system more systematically and understood more about its structures and functions than a control group that read about and memorized the system's parts and functions.[15]
- In a five-week project that used the design of a playground structure to present basic principles of geometry, the CTGV found that fifth-grade students of all ability levels made significant gains in their measurement and scaling skills, scoring well on standard tests of geometric concepts. Thirty-one of the thirty-seven playground designs submitted by students (84 percent) were judged accurate enough to be built—a very high rate of achievement.[16]

Obstacles to Collaborative Inquiry and Design Learning

The research results are quite clear that the benefits of collaborative learning are great, but the research is also very clear that making collaborative team learning work well requires care at a number of points:

- Selecting compatible team members and defining team rules of the road that support positive collaboration
- Choosing group activities that benefit from the differing viewpoints and experiences of team members
- Using discussion strategies to support deeper learning among team members

As Johns Hopkins University's Robert Slavin argues, "It is not enough to simply tell students to work together. They must have a reason to take one another's achievement seriously."

Similar obstacles confront the use of inquiry, design, and project learning approaches. Students unfamiliar with this form of learning must develop readiness skills that enable them to ask relevant and meaningful questions and to create logical arguments. They must also be guided toward being more independent in seeking out answers to questions and researching possible solutions to problems.

To make project approaches work well, teachers must carve out the time to design and plan project activities that match the interests and needs of their students and the school's curriculum, as well as the time for extended project work that doesn't easily fit in the standard fifty-minute classroom period.

Teachers must also learn to play the role of facilitator and coach as well as providing expertise and guidance. In the 21st century, teachers must be comfortable with managing new kinds of classroom dynamics, supporting multiple teams of students working independently as they explore and gain new understandings and skills that will prepare them for 21st century life.

Twenty-first century teachers will also have to be expert at the same 21st century skills they are imparting to their students. Teachers will have to collaborate and communicate with other teachers and experts, working in teams to create and share their best engaging projects that challenge the interests and skill levels of their students and to assess their students' project outcomes.

As noted, the research evidence is conclusive: inquiry, design, and collaborative approaches to learning build a powerful combination of content understanding, basic skills, and applied 21st century skills. However, the research also shows that these methods will require changes in curriculum, instruction, assessment practices, the professional development of teachers, and the learning environments that support 21st century learning.

We turn next to these educational support systems and how they are transforming to meet the demands of the 21st century.

8

Retooling Schooling

RESHAPING SUPPORT SYSTEMS

We need to move beyond subject mastery and increase the rigor
and relevance of education to be competitive in West Virginia,
the United States, and around the world. We're responsible
for producing students who can read and write, but can they
analyze data? Can they solve challenging problems with a first-
rate skill set? Can they communicate effectively? These central
skills are what will make the difference as our global marketplace
grows more and more competitive each day.

—Dr. Steven Paine, West Virginia State Superintendent of Schools

Running a good school is no simple matter. A number of
complex relationships and supporting systems must all work
together to bring the best possible learning experience to each
and every child.

Mapping all the interactions among all the players inside and
outside the school, including students, teachers, administrators,
school boards, curriculum providers, parents and community
members, testing agencies, and more, can result in quite an overwhelming systems diagram, as Figure 8.1 shows.

The P21 framework offers a simpler approach—one that focuses on the five traditional educational support systems familiar to educators and parents alike. To create a 21st century school
system, these interlinked support systems must all work together:

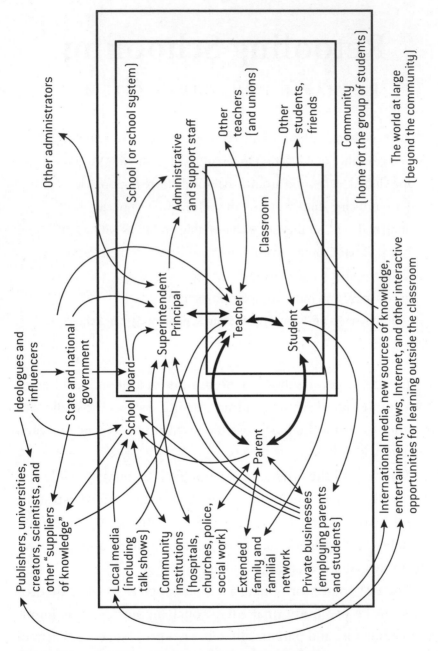

Figure 8.1.   Systems Diagram of School Interactions.

Source: Senge et al., 2000.

- Standards
- Assessments
- Curriculum and instruction
- Professional development
- Learning environments

Figure 8.2 shows these support systems in the context of the entire P21 learning framework.

In this chapter, we first look broadly at how school systems are overhauling their educational systems for the 21st century. Later we dive into each of the support system "pools" in the P21 framework to see how standards, assessments, curriculum and instruction, professional development, and learning environments are

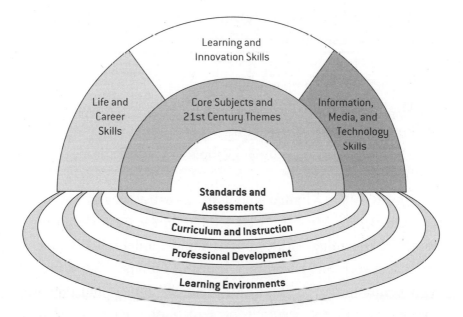

Figure 8.2. **21st Century Learning Framework.**

all shifting to support 21st century learning, understanding, and skills performance. Examples from one school system, West Virginia, provide specifics on one successful approach.

Shifting Systems in Sync

As head of public education for West Virginia, a state known for its beautiful Blue Ridge Mountains and its long association with coal mining, Steve Paine knows that his students need to move forward into the 21st century. So West Virginia got an early start with its 21st Century Learning initiative.[1] The initiative focused on

- Internationally rigorous and relevant curriculum standards (including content, learning skills, and technical tool skills)
- A balanced assessment strategy
- Research-based instructional practices
- A parallel accountability system
- Aligned teacher preparation programs
- The development of a 21st century leadership continuum
- Emphasis on pre-K programs
- The integration of technology tools in every classroom

How will West Virginia schools achieve these goals? How does any school, any district, any state or province, or any nation go about transforming 20th century factory-model school systems into a network of 21st century learning centers? The future of their communities, the health of their economies, and the welfare of their citizens are entirely dependent on preparing each and every child for success in learning, work, and life.

In West Virginia, as in many other school systems working their way toward a 21st century model of teaching and learning, the answer for educators and policymakers lies in incorporating both a systematic approach and a spirit of innovation. They need to take both small, achievable steps and some large leaps in the many components of the education system and to measure progress as they go, course correcting as they learn what works and what doesn't and celebrating their accomplishments along the way.

Many different roads are being traveled in the global movement toward 21st century education systems, but some common patterns and principles are starting to emerge. Looking at a variety of worldwide reports of successful efforts to move toward a 21st century education system, such as the United Kingdom's "Harnessing Technology: Next Generation Learning 2008–14"[2] and the Singapore "Teach Less, Learn More" Initiative,[3] as well as the work of the Partnership for 21st Century Skills, we see six emerging principles that these initiatives all seem to share:

- Vision
- Coordination
- Official policy
- Leadership
- Learning technology
- Teacher learning

Vision

A common and well-articulated vision of 21st century learning needs to be shared among educators, government officials, the business community, parents, and students. This common vision helps the key stakeholders sustain the long-term commitment it takes to transform the education system over time.

To help create that common vision, the P21 Learning Framework, consensus-building activities such as the Four Questions exercise described in the Introduction, effective community information campaigns, and sustained local public communications efforts can all be helpful.

Coordination

All the educational support systems—standards, assessment, curriculum and instruction, professional development, and learning environments—must work together in a coordinated way to support 21st century learning.

Often changes are made in one support system, such as a new curriculum, without coordinated changes being made in all the other linked systems: the learning environment, teacher professional development, aligned assessments and standards, for example. These isolated changes may generate enthusiasm for a while, but without the support necessary from the other systems to sustain the change, they almost always become short-lived "experiments."

Official Policy

Successful initiatives that are making 21st century education improvements stick have their new innovations codified into the education systems' governing policy documents; into the official learning standards, goals, and objectives; and into the assessment and accountability practices required by the governing education authority (more on each of these systems shortly).

Additionally, sustainable initiatives commit adequate funding during the transformation period—at least five to seven years, and sometimes more. Funding needs to support the long-term planning and phased implementation of such a large-scale change initiative. This funding commitment mostly involves shifting existing funding to new activities, though some additional funding for teacher development and improved technology infrastructure is likely to be needed during the transition to a 21st century model.

These measures help ensure that changes in everyday teaching methods, the curriculum, and the learning environment of a school will continue to work in concert toward supporting solid 21st century learning goals, and that there will be time and resources for learning innovations to take hold and be refined.

Leadership

Developing a successful 21st century education program requires both distributed and coordinated leadership. Authority and decision making must rest with those most capable of making a good decision, and technology must be used to communicate and coordinate action efficiently. Those involved need to take the time to learn from each other's experiences (successes and setbacks) as new methods and processes are innovated.

As a result, education leaders at all levels (national, state or province, district, school, and classroom) must firmly and consistently lead all stakeholders—students, parents, teachers, administrators, government officials, community members—toward the same 21st century learning goals of rigorous and relevant knowledge, understanding, and proficiency in 21st century skills. All these leaders must also openly and frequently communicate progress toward these goals and encourage experimentation and innovations in creating a successful 21st century education system.

Learning Technology

Providing students easy access to the Internet in the classroom, as well as to laptop computers, handheld devices, and other learning technologies, is a vital part of any 21st century education redesign. But the technology must also be focused on supporting each student's 21st century learning goals.

Administrative technology (student information databases, assessment tracking systems, school portals, class management systems, parent communications, video monitoring, and the like) should be used to automate much of the administrivia of running a school or education system, freeing time and resources to support quality teaching and effective 21st century student learning.

Teacher Learning

In all successful transformations, professional development of both new and practicing teachers is a top priority of education leaders. Teachers must become 21st century learners themselves, learning from inquiry, design, and collaborative approaches that build a strong community of professional educators.

Teachers, whether they are fresh out of an education school or have been in the classroom for twenty years, must learn to develop their design, coaching, and facilitating skills to guide and support their students' learning projects. Teachers must continually sharpen their skills at using the power of learning technologies to help deepen understanding and further develop 21st century skills.

These teaching methods are a break from the past. They have not been commonly taught in schools of education or widely available in teacher professional development programs. Yet the rising demand for 21st century skills and the teaching methods that build them are rapidly changing this situation; education schools such as Columbia Teachers College in New York City and many teacher professional development programs around the world are shifting toward a 21st century teacher education model that includes practice in designing and implementing inquiry, design, and collaborative learning projects, bringing many more opportunities for teachers to master 21st century teaching methods.

Support Systems

Each of the traditional educational support systems is being reshaped to help build successful 21st century schools and learning communities. The following sections review some of the progress being made in these systems.

Standards

Standards are designed to answer the question: What should our children be learning? Standards documents in the 20th century were typically long lists of the content students *should know* in a certain subject at a certain age or grade level.

For the 21st century, standards emphasize what students *should be able to do with this content*—defining the skills students can employ when applying the content to useful work in each subject area. These 21st century standards also include levels of mastery for a given standard, from novice level to expert.

For example, Table 8.1 shows part of a redesigned 21st century Content Standard for Grade 5 Science from the West Virginia learning standards.

Though approaches to standards vary around the world, there has been a trend in the last decade to create very detailed standards that cover a huge number of content topics. In these "mile-wide and inch-deep"[4] standards it has been estimated that in some cases it would take as many as twenty-two years of schooling to adequately teach all the content identified in a set of elementary school standards documents!

It could also take a long time to test students' knowledge of all this content—so test designers test only a small fraction of the standards each year, changing which items they test every year.

In many ways, standards have been designed for the way we test. Standards have been limited to the types of knowledge best tested by the multiple-choice questions on the machine-scored tests so commonly used to measure student progress.

This has led teachers to focus on "coverage," superficially rushing through a vast number of topics with their students, and to emphasize memorization and recall in preparation for the end-of-year, high-stakes standards-based tests that determine so much of a student's future learning path.[5]

Table 8.1. Grade 5 Science Standard from West Virginia.

Grade 5	Science
Standard 3:	Application of Science
SC.S.5.3	Students will Explore the relationship between the parts and the whole system; construct a variety of useful models; examine changes that occur in an object or system. Demonstrate an understanding of the interdependence between science and technology. Demonstrate the ability to utilize technology to gather data and communicate designs, results, and conclusions. Demonstrate the ability to evaluate the impact of different points of view on health, population, resources, and environmental practices.

Performance Descriptors SC.PD.5.3

Distinguished	Above Mastery	Mastery	Partial Mastery	Novice
Fifth-grade students at the distinguished level evaluate the role of parts that contribute to the functioning of a model; identify an innovation with the science that makes it possible; select and use the appropriate technology to collect scientific data; use multiple media sources to evaluate different points of view regarding health, population, resources, and environmental practices.	Fifth-grade students at the above mastery level analyze parts as they contribute to the functioning of a model; match an innovation with the science that makes it possible; identify and use the appropriate technology to collect scientific data; compare media sources to evaluate two different points of view regarding health, population, resources, and environmental practices.	Fifth-grade students at the mastery level compare the functioning of parts to the functioning of a model; report on a technological innovation; use the appropriate technology to collect scientific data; use two media sources to evaluate points of view regarding health, population, resources, or environmental practices.	Fifth-grade students at the partial mastery level explain the function of parts of a model; identify a technological innovation; use technology to collect scientific data; identify the point of view of a media source regarding health, population, resources, or environmental practices.	Fifth-grade students at the novice level identify the parts of a model; identify a technological innovation; use a technology to collect data; recognize that media sources have a point of view regarding health, population, resources, or environmental practices.

Though many schools in many countries have begun moving in a more 21st century direction, this teach-to-the-test trend has truly been a global phenomenon. A recent international survey of teachers in twenty-three countries in North America, Europe, Asia, Latin America, and Africa found that the three most common teaching practices in schools were filling out worksheets, having students individually working at the same pace and sequence on the same tasks, and answering tests.[6]

This leaves little time for deep dives into topics, for depth of understanding, or for the mastery of the 21st century skills, and almost no time for collaborative explorations of questions, issues, or real-world problems that might engage students in their learning.

So how do we move from this 20th century standards model to a 21st century model?

As they say in Singapore, "Teach Less, Learn More." Focus the standards on a short list of the big ideas in each subject area. Make sure that often-neglected topics that have real-world relevance for students are included (statistics and probabilities in math, the human-made world of technology in science, and the like). And include and embed 21st century skills as part of the learning standards.

As an example, here are three of West Virginia's Grades 5–8 21st Century Skills Standards:

Standard 1: Information and Communication Skills: The student will access, analyze, manage, integrate, evaluate, and create information in a variety of forms using appropriate technology skills and communicate that information in an appropriate oral, written, or multimedia format.

Standard 2: Thinking and Reasoning Skills: The student will demonstrate the ability to explore and develop new ideas, to intentionally apply sound reasoning processes and to frame, analyze and solve complex problems using appropriate technology tools.

Standard 3: Personal and Workplace Skills: The student will exhibit leadership, ethical behavior, respect for others; accept responsibility for personal actions considering the impact on others; take the initiative to plan and execute tasks; and interact productively as a member of a group.

Standards should focus on real-world problems that promote learning across the disciplines using 21st century themes and interdisciplinary issues. Incorporating fast-developing cross-discipline areas of knowledge, such as bioengineering and green energy technologies, will help develop the skills needed for the kinds of career opportunities likely to be available when students enter the job market.

Standards also need to be designed such that the depth increases as students progress through the grade levels, investigating various aspects of a "big idea" over time. This way, understanding builds on earlier work and skill mastery increases over time. An example would be learning about ancient Greek culture in Grade 4, Athenian democracy in Grade 8, and comparative Greek and other political philosophies and practices in Grade 12.

Multiple methods must be used to assess performance on the standards, especially on 21st century skills performance. These assessment methods may include evaluations of portfolios of student project work, classroom observations and performance rubrics, online quizzes and simulation-based assessments, juried presentations, and juried exhibits or performances.

Assessments

> The problem is not that teachers teach to the test, but that teachers need tests worth teaching to.
> —Lauren and Daniel Resnick, 1992

Assessment of student skills and knowledge is essential to guide learning and provide feedback to both students and teachers on how well they are all doing in reaching desired 21st century learning goals.

"You get what you measure" is often said about educational assessment, and the decades-long trend toward narrow, high-stakes tests of content knowledge in a few subject areas (language arts, math, science, and social studies) has made another saying popular: "Teach to the test."

Recent standards and assessment practices have focused students on memorizing the content that will be required for high-stakes exams. These often-stressful exams can determine the future learning and career path of a student and are also used (and often misused) to judge the quality of an entire school and the educators in it.

The strong focus on after-instruction tests, or *summative assessments,* has downplayed the value of during-instruction evaluations, *or formative assessments.* Formative assessments, like quizzes and lab reports, are often called "assessments *for* learning," as opposed to summative "assessments *of* learning." Formative assessments can be more valuable to both students and teachers than summative ones, as they provide feedback in real time and allow for quick adjustments in instruction to better meet the students' immediate learning needs.

The focus on high-stakes summative tests has also deemphasized the value of a whole range of other more authentic assessment methods from extended essays and peer- and self-evaluations to project work judged by evaluation rubrics or by a panel of experts (like the SARS Web site in the ThinkQuest competition described earlier).

Sadly, students who have special learning needs, have difficulty in reading, or are second-language learners often perform poorly on all the standardized multiple choice tests because these tests are so dependent on reading skills. Though accommodations do exist, many special needs students are simply left out of the assessment process.

What has also been glaringly left out in recent assessment practice is the measurement of essential 21st century skills and the deeper understandings and applied knowledge that can come from rigorous learning projects.

So how do we move to a new balance of 21st century assessments that provide useful feedback on students' progress in understanding a learning topic or their gains in 21st century skills, as well as measuring a much wider range of capacities and abilities that better reflect the whole learner?

We need better summative tests and formative evaluations that measure a combination of content knowledge, basic skills, higher-order thinking skills, deeper comprehension and understanding, applied knowledge, and 21st century skills performance. Evaluations embedded into ongoing learning activities that provide timely feedback and suggest additional learning activities that can improve understanding and performance would also be very helpful.

If a single test measures both basic and applied skills, there is no need for *more* tests, just *better* tests that measure more of what students need for success in the 21st century.[7]

Figure 8.3 shows an example from a West Virginia Grade 11 Social Studies summative test item that moves beyond measuring memorized facts. To lower costs, this test is being delivered electronically instead of on paper.

Another good example of a more authentic 21st century assessment is the College Work and Readiness Assessment (CWRA), developed by the Council for Aid to Education and the RAND Corporation. Students use research reports, budgets, and other documents to help craft an answer to a complex problem, such as how to manage traffic congestion caused by population growth. As one ninth-grade student said after taking the CWRA test, "I proposed a new transportation system for the city—it's expensive, but it will cut pollution."[8]

We need to use a wide variety of real-time formative assessments that measure content knowledge, basic and higher-order thinking skills, comprehension and understanding, and applied 21st century skills performance. Many effective methods to assess ongoing learning progress are available; here are just a few:

- Extended student essays
- Observation rubrics on a teacher's handheld device
- Online instant polls, quizzes, voting, and blog commentaries

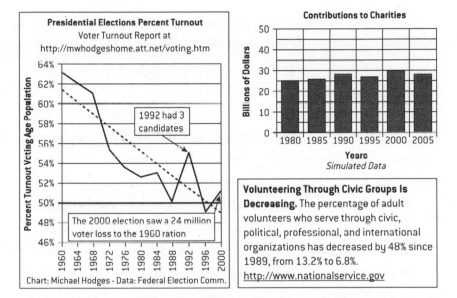

Grade 11—Citizenship

SS.0.11.01.03 **analyze** the changing nature of civic responsibility

Depth of knowledge 3

Directions: The mayor of your town was asked to speak at a school assembly on citizenship. As part of her presentation, she shared the following charts and information with the eleventh graders at your school. Based on her presentation, fill in the circle next to the best answer for **Question 8.**

Presidential Elections Percent Turnout

Voter Turnout Report at
http://mwhodgeshome.att.net/voting.htm

1992 had 3 candidates

The 2000 election saw a 24 million voter loss to the 1960 ration

Chart: Michael Hodges - Data: Federal Election Comm.

Contributions to Charities

Simulated Data

Volunteering Through Civic Groups Is Decreasing. The percentage of adult volunteers who serve through civic, political, professional, and international organizations has decreased by 48% since 1989, from 13.2% to 6.8%.
http://www.nationalservice.gov

Question 8: Which of the following hypotheses would best introduce an analysis of the above data?

Ⓐ All forms of civic participation have shown a considerable decline.

Ⓑ Even though the amounts of charitable giving have held fairly consistent, civic engagement in other areas has shown a significant decrease.

Ⓒ Civic participation requiring an individual's time is more prevalent than passive participation.

Ⓓ No conclusions can be drawn from the data presented.

Figure 8.3.   West Virginia Grade 11 Social Studies Test Question.

- Progress tracked in solving online simulation challenges and design problems
- Portfolio evaluations of current project work and mid-project reviews
- Expert evaluations of ongoing internship and service work in the community

Collections of formative assessments can also be used as part of a summative evaluation, offering a rich set of multiple measures as the basis for an end-of-project or end-of-unit assessment of progress toward learning goals and standards.

Technology-based assessments can automate some of the labor-intensive tasks of assessing student performance and offer new ways to evaluate skills performance, especially through the use of problem scenarios and simulations based on real-world situations.

Because assessments tend to drive all the rest of the education support systems, a number of promising national and global initiatives are under way to design a core set of balanced 21st century assessments that truly align with the kinds of deeper understanding and skills performance so needed in our times. These 21st century assessments promise to provide a much broader picture of the full capabilities of the "whole child"—including the cognitive, emotional, physical, social, and ethical aspects of a healthy, safe, engaged, supported, and positively challenged student.[9]

Curriculum and Instruction

So far we have discussed a number of features of effective 21st century learning methods and a model of a 21st century approach to instruction using inquiry, design, and collaborative learning projects. A curriculum based on a blend of these learning methods with more direct forms of instruction is what is now needed to build knowledge, understanding, creativity, and other 21st century skills.

An encouraging sign that 21st century learning methods are taking hold is the recent announcement that the Massachusetts Institute of Technology (MIT) has stopped presenting introductory physics in large-lecture format (more than three hundred students) and is instead having small student teams do hands-on labs, interactive computer-based activities, and video-based minilectures. As a result, class attendance is up and the course failure rate has dropped by 50 percent.[10]

So what should shift in curriculum and instruction to reach a new 21st century balance?

A reasonable goal for most education systems moving from a 20th century model to a 21st century one might be 50 percent time for inquiry, design, and collaborative project learning and 50 percent for more traditional and direct methods of instruction. Once this goal is achieved, more and more of the direct instruction will occur in the context of questions and problems that arise in learning projects and need addressing so that students can move their project work forward. The lessons delivered this way gain greater relevance and are more likely to be remembered.

Designing and sequencing engaging learning projects so that they meet learning standards and increasingly deepen understanding and build 21st century skills as a student progresses through school will be a challenge for many education systems. Fortunately, a growing number of online libraries and repositories contain a wealth of effective learning projects that will be helpful in developing this type of multi-year project- or unit-based curriculum. (See Appendix A.)

Online and distance learning courses, also based on a project approach, can supplement a school's curriculum, especially where local teachers aren't available to teach certain courses.

Teacher Professional Development

The success of the 21st century skills movement depends on altering what goes on each day in the world's classrooms and schools. Teachers are the front line in this change, and they must have the knowledge, skills, and support to be effective 21st century teachers.

Teacher professional development programs, for both new teachers-in-training and working teachers, are taking up the challenge. They have begun providing the learning experiences necessary to prepare teachers to incorporate inquiry, design, and collaborative project teaching methods and to use technology and assessments of 21st century skills effectively in their everyday classroom work.

One good example of a concerted effort to bring 21st century learning approaches to a large teacher community is West Virginia's effort to teach project learning methods to all the teachers in the state. Using a variety of professional development offerings including the Intel Teach program and Oracle Education Foundation's Project Learning Institute (a video documentary on this Institute and the resulting project is available on the included DVD and on the book's Web site), as well as state and district-developed programs, West Virginia teachers are

A West Virginia Teacher's Success Project

In 2007 fifth-grade teacher Deb Austin Brown of St. Albans Elementary joined eighty educators from around the globe to learn how to design and lead engaging learning projects that build 21st century skills and deepen understanding of school subjects. She learned how to lead and support all the phases of a learning project: define, plan, do, review, and manage through the project cycle.

With the help of other teachers from around the world and an online project environment with tools and digital space to hold all the project work, Deb designed what she called The Success Project. Students chose a successful historical or contemporary leader, researched what helped make that leader a success, and created Web pages that captured their findings. They received feedback and comments on their Web pages from other students around the world (students of some of the international teachers Deb met in the training). They then presented their findings to other students, teachers, parents, and community leaders at a school exhibition.

Ryan, one of Deb's highly engaged and ambitious fifth-grade students, continued developing his success skills by interviewing a prominent high-tech business leader in the community, and even the governor of West Virginia.

Deb's Success Project certainly empowered Ryan to be a more successful 21st century learner and a future leader.

honing their own 21st century skills as they learn how to teach these skills to their students.

Successful professional development programs that give teachers the knowledge, tools, and practice to be effective 21st century teachers have a number of common characteristics.[11] These programs tend to be

- Experiential, engaging teachers in the concrete tasks of designing, implementing, managing, and assessing learning activities and projects, and observing other teachers' methods and skills, which helps to clarify their own values and beliefs in what makes learning effective
- Grounded in a teacher's own questions, problems, issues, and challenges, as well as what professional research has to offer
- Collaborative, using the collective experience and expertise of other teachers and the wider community of educators exploring 21st century learning methods
- Connected to a teacher's own work with students and the teacher's curriculum and school culture, as well as connected with technology to the wider world of learning
- Sustained and intensive, with ongoing support by modeling, coaching, mentoring, and collaborative problem solving with other teachers and administrators on issues of teaching practice
- Integrated with all other aspects of school change, reform, and transformation

Strong, continuous investments in 21st century teacher professional development will be essential to the transformation of education systems around the globe. They will need to be well coordinated with ongoing changes in curriculum, assessment, standards, and the overall learning environment.

Learning Environments

A 21st century learning environment includes a number of important elements that work together to support 21st century teaching and learning:

- The physical buildings, classrooms, and facilities, and their design
- A school's daily operations, scheduling, courses, and activities
- The educational technology infrastructure
- The professional community of teachers, administrators, and others
- The culture of the school
- Community involvement and participation
- The education system's leadership and policies

To support the unique learning needs of each child and to create the conditions in which 21st century learning can best happen, new learning structures, tools, and relationships must be created. Building 21st century "whole environments for the whole child" involves changes in the educational use of space and time, technology, and communities and leadership.[12]

Learning Space and Time Learning in the 21st century is expanding the boundaries of space and time. As access to the Internet grows, more learning is happening online, after school, at home, in libraries and cafés. Learning is becoming an anytime, anyplace activity, more woven into all the parts of everyday life.

The physical environments for learning—school buildings and facilities—must also meet the challenge of becoming more flexible, to accommodate a wider variety of student, teacher, and technology interactions and activities, as illustrated in Figure 8.4.

Space for project work, group presentations, individual study and research, teamwork at a computer, performance spaces, labs and workshops for experiments and design projects, and areas for sports and recreation must all be accommodated in 21st century school designs. A flexible "learning studio" approach that can be reconfigured when needed will be an important part of the blueprint for 21st century learning.

These classrooms and school facilities will also have to tackle the challenge of becoming "green"—being more environmentally

Figure 8.4. New Learning Environments.

responsible in the use of energy and materials. This presents a wonderful opportunity to use the school environment itself as a learning laboratory for improving energy efficiency and water conservation, and for growing food in school gardens and mini- farms to be used in school and community meals.

Schools can also become learning centers for the surrounding community, and as they do, community use of the school facilities will become an important design goal for schools. Schools as community learning and service centers, with health, child care, family, social, cultural, gardening, hobby, and recreational services available on the same campus, is an important trend that will only grow as schools move to incorporate more authentic community-based learning projects into their daily schedules. The community comes to the school, and the school becomes more a vital part of community life. A large number of successful examples of community schools are already in action, including many in Chicago, Houston, and Philadelphia;[13] others in countries with strong national investments in social and education programs like Denmark, Holland, Finland, Sweden, and France; and in rural areas in developing countries across the world, where schools can serve as the social and cultural hub for the village.

Flexibility in the use of time will also be a challenge to the operational design of schools. The agrarian calendar with summers off and the industrial fifty-minute period marked by ringing bells will give way to flexible schedules, year-round schools, open after-school and weekend hours, and time for extended project work and community service activities. Time for teachers to collaborate and plan rich learning activities and projects will also be an essential part of a 21st century school calendar.

Learning with Technology   Unquestionably, technology can provide great benefits to learners, supporting their development of 21st century skills and knowledge. In 21st century schools, a robust technology infrastructure that can handle a wide variety of digital learning tools and devices with always-on access to the broadband Internet will be as important as electricity, lighting, and running water. Research has shown that student learning gains are greatest when technology is seamlessly integrated with rich learning content, sound principles of learning, high-quality teaching, and an aligned system of assessments, standards, and quality learning experiences geared to the needs of each child.[14] The challenge now is to apply the right tools for the right learning task from the wildly expanding list of learning technologies and tools. Mobile tools will be especially important in this anyplace, anytime learning world, along with the ability for students, groups, and teachers to keep all their work safely stored, organized, and easily accessible online.

As noted, our net generation digital-native learners can help support each other and their teachers in the best use of technology for learning activities and projects in the 21st century curriculum. Students and teachers will work more as a team (and—with parents, siblings, and other community members involved—more as a whole learning community) in determining the best learning paths and tools to support each student's learning program.

The learning and thinking power tools of our times and of the times to come are well suited for the kinds of learning experiences most needed to develop 21st century skills—the inquiry, design, and collaborative learning projects that deal with real-world problems, issues, questions, and challenges.

Learning Communities and Leadership It can take more than a village these days to educate a child.

The network of people and resources involved in providing educational opportunities to a child can be truly global, as the story in the sidebar "Keys to the 21st Century Learning Community" illustrates. The story is also documented in a video on the DVD included with this book and on this book's Web site at www.21stcenturybook.com.

Harry from Ghana was supported and encouraged by family members, by his teachers and school administrators, by his student teammates in other countries, by educators from around the world who judged his work and gave him feedback, and by international foundations and government agencies that sponsored educational competitions.

Through determination, a supportive school community, and the concerted application of a number of 21st century skills, Harry was able to engage in a global learning community and find opportunities to further his own learning and career.

Learning environments across the globe will increasingly provide these kinds of opportunities to students. Students everywhere will be a part of an open, global learning community with strong local leadership that creates a culture of opportunity, trust, and caring.

Similarly, successful 21st century education leaders will be those who focus on the learning needs of each student and who provide the support needed by their entire professional learning community—teachers, administrators, and parents. They will be leaders who are always outward looking, searching for new learning opportunities in the world outside their school or country,

Keys to the 21st Century Learning Community

Harry grew up in a village on the outskirts of Kumasi, a city north of Ghana's coastal capital, Accra. His local high school was just introducing computers into the curriculum when he entered. Harry was not sure about these machines at first, but eventually he understood just what a computer could do and suddenly he saw his future before him.

To Harry, the computer was the digital key to connecting to the rest of the world, and a passport to greater opportunities than his village could provide. He also saw that he could help other students like himself take hold of this key and use it to better their lives.

With the encouragement of his computer teacher, Harry entered a Think-Quest competition and helped create a Web site on sea mammals. But without a computer of his own (a very expensive item in Ghana), Harry had to walk miles on a bush trail each day to the only Internet café within reach and use his small allowance to pay for computer time. He worked online for months with students from the United States and Australia. When he found out his team had won an award, Harry was thrilled—all his hard work had paid off.

Harry went on to enter a number of other Web-based competitions, still without a computer of his own, hoping to eventually have enough money from prizes in these competitions to buy his own computer. Harry continued to help other students in Ghana learn how to communicate, collaborate, and learn with computers, as he worked on developing better and better Web sites. One competition brought Harry to the United States to receive a "Doors to Diplomacy" award from the U.S. State Department.

Harry was invited to speak about his experience in using technology to learn 21st century skills at a ThinkQuest meeting around the time of his U.S. trip. After his presentation, Harry was stunned to see his wish granted—in celebration of his achievements despite the tremendous challenges he faced, Harry was presented a laptop computer of his own.

Harry has continued his career in helping others in his country and around the world use technology to open doors to learning and opportunity.

and who demonstrate caring for the well-being and whole development of their students and staff.[15]

Successful education leaders will also build partnerships with businesses, foundations, nonprofit educational organizations, community groups, and other schools and educational institutions across the globe. This will bring new opportunities for their students and teachers to collaborate and learn from a world of experts and other learners, preparing them for work and life in the truly global village of the 21st century.

From Skills to Expertise: Future Learning Frameworks

Designing, redesigning, creating, and re-creating the education systems that will support 21st century learning will not be easy, and there will be many difficult obstacles to surmount as we move through a time of great change and great opportunity in the world.

We are fortunate to have a large and growing number of schools, school networks, states, countries, and enthusiastic and committed education leaders and teachers that have already achieved a great deal of progress in moving education into the 21st century. Their pioneering efforts to chart new paths for learning provide us with hope, confidence, and inspiration that we can achieve a better way of learning that better prepares our children for our times and the times to come.

However, a century is a long time, and change is the only dependable constant. As we move through the 21st century, we will need to invent new learning solutions, new school designs, and new ways to prepare our students for the future—21st century learning is clearly a work in progress.

As Alan Kay, a particularly farsighted technologist and educator, once said, "The best way to predict the future is to invent it."

As discussed in Chapter One, expertise is highly valued in a knowledge-and-innovation society. Figure 8.5 recaps its place as the most critical link in the value chain of 21st century work.

In the 21st century, learning can be viewed as using the best methods available to produce a wide variety of experts with deep understanding and the ability to successfully apply what they know to the important questions and problems of our times.

But exactly what makes an expert different from a novice?

Thanks to decades of research in cognitive psychology, neuroscience, and other learning sciences, we have a great deal of "expertise on expertise"—knowledge of how experts think and use their knowledge and skills.[16] We now know that experts

- Notice important patterns and features that novices miss—like climatologists connecting increasing amounts of atmospheric carbon dioxide with rising global temperatures
- Have an extensive internal database of content knowledge and experience organized around powerful principles and deep understandings—such as a lawyer who knows the

Knowledge Age Value Chain

Data → Information → Knowledge → **Expertise** → Marketing → Services (and Products)

Figure 8.5   Knowledge Age Value Chain.

significant parts of case law that relate to a consumer safety
lawsuit
- Can easily select from their deep knowledge base just those
  facts, principles, and processes most applicable to the
  problem or issue at hand—such as a doctor knowing just
  the right combination of treatments for a certain type of
  lung infection
- Can retrieve the relevant parts of their knowledge quickly
  and without much mental effort—like a seasoned auto
  mechanic who can instantly diagnose a car's problem from
  the sounds its engine makes

We also know that experts use the power of learning tools
and technologies in more effective and efficient ways than novices. Experts use their digital thinking tools to continually expand,
organize, and deepen their expertise and to help apply their
knowledge and skills to new and more complex challenges.

Experts are often quite passionate about their field of expertise. They share common motivations, values, attitudes, and beliefs
with others in their professional community and care deeply
about the issues and dilemmas that challenge their profession.
Knowledge, skills, thinking tools, motivations, values, attitudes,
beliefs, communities of practice, and professional identity—all
are vital parts of an expert's world.

As we move further along into the 21st century, engaged and
passionate learners and teachers will share more of these expert
qualities and will model their learning after the learning practices
of experts.

So how will this affect our current 21st century learning frameworks and models?

The distinctions between knowledge and skills in the current P21 rainbow model may give way to a more holistic model that puts the learner at the center of increasingly wider concentric rings of learning support, as shown in Figure 8.6.

In this model, "whole learners" with all their developing facets of expertise—knowledge, skills, motivations, values, attitudes, beliefs, feelings, health, safety, resilience, and other qualities—are placed at the center.

Learners are immediately surrounded by those who influence their learning most—other students and peers, parents, family, teachers, experts, and the rest.

Whole learning environments—the entire collection of places, tools, technologies, community resources, informal education spaces like museums and art studios, and formal educational supports such as learning standards, assessments, teacher professional development, leadership and educational policy—are all parts of the next ring of the model.

Learning communities and learning societies are the next two outward rings. The networks of people, places, and objects that accompany students on their learning travels are the main components of learning communities, and learning societies are a country's national (and increasingly international) educational institutions and cultural services that support a student's education.

The concentric rings of this model are set in the larger world of learning—the physical worlds of experience and the mental worlds of knowledge, skills, and expertise.

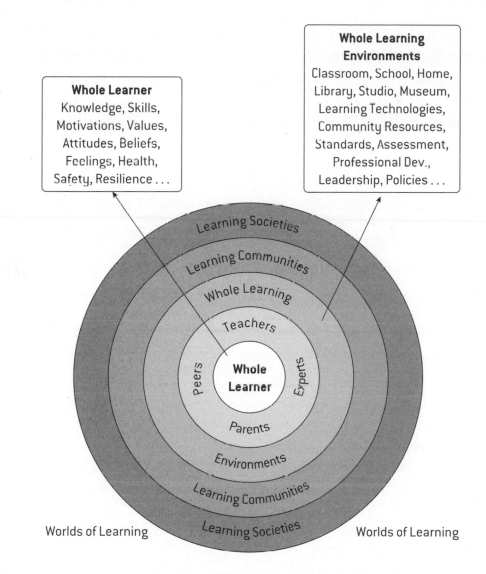

Whole Learner
Knowledge, Skills,
Motivations, Values,
Attitudes, Beliefs,
Feelings, Health,
Safety, Resilience . . .

**Whole Learning
Environments**
Classroom, School, Home,
Library, Studio, Museum,
Learning Technologies,
Community Resources,
Standards, Assessment,
Professional Dev.,
Leadership, Policies . . .

Learning Societies

Learning Communities

Whole Learning

Teachers

Peers **Whole
Learner** Experts

Parents

Environments

Learning Communities

Worlds of Learning   Learning Societies   Worlds of Learning

Figure 8.6.   Possible Future 21st Century Learning Framework.

As we move further into the 21st century, more and more countries will put more and more emphasis on learning. They will embed learning experiences into all aspects of life and culture and become learning societies that put a high-quality education for all their citizens at the top of the list of their nation's priorities.

9

Conclusion

LEARNING FOR LIFE— BUILDING A BETTER WORLD

Since we live in an age of innovation, a practical education must prepare a person for work that does not yet exist and cannot yet be clearly defined.
—Peter Drucker

The real source of wealth and capital in this new era is not material things. It is the human mind, the human spirit, the human imagination, and our faith in the future.
—Steve Forbes

Our news is now zoomed to our screens from every corner of the planet. Our phone calls hop along a global inter-linked communications grid. Our money tumbles through a global electronic financial network. Our businesses work 24/7 with teams scattered across time zones. Our consumer products are pieced together in a global supply chain. Our national economies are wound together into one global complex. And our students are connecting with each other around the globe.

We have entered a time in history where all sorts of borders and boundaries are vanishing into thin air, and we are facing the reality that "we are all passengers on one very large spaceship," as the visionary Buckminster Fuller was fond of saying.

Education has come to the global party a bit late, but it is catching up fast. Education leaders in many countries now have the business community and government officials on their side—education is now seen as the golden ticket to a brighter economic future.

How well we educate our children—whether or not they learn the skills now needed to participate and thrive in our global economy—will determine the future health, wealth, and welfare of everyone.

Our recent global recession has given us a painful glimpse of what life could be like if we don't succeed in providing our children a 21st century education. Though the causes of the global recession are not directly related to education, the results provide us with an important lesson.

The painful recession that has left so many without work and with much less to live on can serve as a grim warning of what it could be like to have a nation of 20th century educated citizens in a 21st century world. There are many countries in the world where this kind of economic depression has long been a part of everyday life, where living on a dollar a day or less is the norm.

No one wants a depressed economy, a low standard of living, an unproductive economy, few social services, or depressed and struggling families with little hope—this is not the future any nation needs or wants.

The best insurance against this sad fate and our best hope for a brighter and more prosperous future is to continue to invest in providing a 21st century education for all our children, even in difficult economic times. Whether living in India, Indiana, Indonesia, Ireland, Iran, Israel, Iceland, or Italy, all students need to learn the same 21st century skills to secure a good job and contribute to their community.

Since every country can share a common vision of what a 21st century education is and can work toward a similar set of learning goals and methods, every country can contribute to a global pool of expertise on how best to implement a 21st century education system. This will mean that an investment that produces a successful learning innovation in one country can have a large-scale effect as many other countries adopt and adapt the innovation for their own use.

With increased international educational cooperation and collaboration (an essential 21st century skill!) every country can play a part in building a global learning network as powerful and pervasive as our existing business, financial, and communications global networks.

As we have seen, students across the globe are already networking and learning from each other, connecting, sharing, and collaborating on all sorts of learning projects and activities. Our net generation students are helping to invent this new global learning network each day as they experience the freedom and joy of learning without borders.

We have already come a long way toward societies where learning is deeply woven into the fabric of everyday life; where digital devices in our pockets give us answers to our questions and connect us to our friends in a couple of clicks; where schools and colleges are becoming vibrant learning and community service centers for our neighborhoods and villages; where collaborative learning activities and projects are more a part of our homes, museums, cafés, and community centers than ever before; where bookstores, home improvement stores, and computer stores are offering classes and tutoring in their own learning centers; where much of our time at work is spent learning to become better experts and innovators.

We can look forward to a time when a powerful global learning network of 21st century schools and online learning services will provide opportunities for all children, no matter where they live, to have a quality 21st century education, and to acquire the 21st century skills and expertise needed for a successful work life, a happy family life, an active community life, and a lifetime of enjoyable learning.

There is much good work to be done to help make this a 21st century global reality for us all. Consider the following recent examples:

- Jewish, Moslem, and Christian students at the School for Peace in Israel created a video showing their various perspectives on the possibilities for Middle East peace. They invited students from other schools to a workshop at their multicultural school, showed the video, and helped their teachers lead dialogs on positive actions each student can take in the struggle for peace.
- Students in a Palo Alto, California, high school robotics class researched the needs of quadriplegics and the mobility-challenged. They designed a "LaserFinger" device that uses a head-mounted laser to turn on electric appliances and devices—and are devising a plan for a high-tech manufacturing company and a national disability organization to provide these LaserFingers free to all that need them.

- Teams of elementary students in the Netherlands created landscape designs for the front of their school that included trees, perennial shrubs, and a drought-resistant vegetable garden. Detailed budgets and work plans are included in their designs. The designs were judged by gardening and landscaping experts and the top-scoring plan was awarded city funds for the students and community volunteers to implement their design.

- High school science students in Sydney joined classrooms around the world in taking a variety of local environmental measurements and uploading their data to a worldwide database that tracks global climate change trends. The students also assisted a local environmental organization in doing free energy audits of homes in their neighborhoods, distributing energy conservation information, and helping residents install free compact fluorescent light bulbs.

- After a close call between a car and student on a bicycle at an intersection near their school in London, middle school students in a civics class measured the traffic flow at different times of the day, took videos of the activity in the intersection, and prepared a detailed plan, report, and proposal for a traffic light at the intersection. They presented their data and arguments for the proposal to the city council and the council voted to install the new traffic light.

As you can see, students are making a difference in our 21st century world.

As more schools and educational programs embrace problem- and design-oriented learning projects, educators, parents, and civic leaders are discovering that students are capable of doing much more than anyone thought they ever could.

Time after time, students prove that they can dive into the depths of a real-world problem, apply their 21st century skills to devise innovative solutions, and become expert on the subject, all at the same time.

It seems that children are natural-born problem seekers and solvers.

And if the problems are ones that they really care about, ones that affect their lives and the lives of their friends and family, there are few limits to what students will learn to help solve the problem.

What are these big "glocal"—global and local—21st century problems that we all face at home and across the world?

Figure 9.1 sets them out: the big "E" problems of our new era.

Getting a good education, a decent job and income in a healthy economy, having affordable and sustainable energy and a healthy environment, and doing all we can to eliminate poverty, the lack of equity between rich and poor and the conflicts in the world caused by such disparities—these are the big issues of our 21st century era.

And at the center is our quality of life, including the quality of our health care, both physical and mental. In Bhutan this would be called our "Gross National Happiness" or GNH.

Harnessing students' passion to solve local versions of these global issues that define our quality of life may be one of the best ways we have to fully engage students in their learning, build 21st century skills, cultivate meaningful and memorable knowledge, and actively apply learning to useful work.

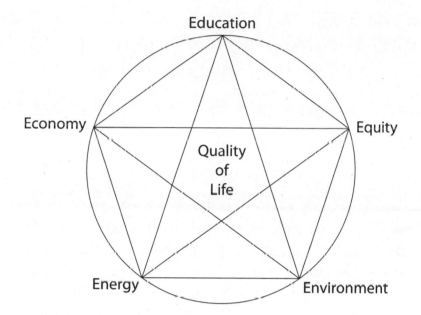

Figure 9.1. The "Big E" Global Problems.

Given the challenges of our times, our students will need plenty of practice in using their 21st century skills to be better problem solvers and innovators, and the world could certainly use some passionate and creative problem solvers right now!

It's time to give all our students the chance to learn how to build a better world.

APPENDIX A

Resources

To help illustrate and support the main themes of this book, there are a number of resources you may find helpful in your travels down the road to 21st century learning.

21st Century Skills Example Videos DVD

The video DVD included at the back of this book contains living examples of classrooms and educational programs that are successfully developing 21st century skills and knowledge.

These video case studies were selected to highlight how teachers and students are tackling real-world problems, learning rigorous content knowledge, and building their proficiency in 21st century skills, all through engaging and challenging learning projects.

The DVD includes eight documentary studies:

1. The California Propositions Public Services Announcement Project from the Metropolitan Arts and Technology High School, an Envision school in San Francisco, California. (Courtesy of the Pearson Foundation.)
   a. Overview of the project
   b. Skill-by-skill descriptions

2. 21st Century Skills Assessment from the Napa New Technology High School, a New Technology school in Napa, California. (Courtesy of the Pearson Foundation.)

3. The Culture of 21st Century Skills from High Tech High, one of the High Tech High schools in San Diego, California. (Courtesy of the Pearson Foundation.)

4. The Science Lab (Biology) Project from the School of the Future, a Coalition of Essential Schools member school in New York City. (Courtesy of the Coalition of Essential Schools.)

5. The SARS Project from the ThinkQuest Program, with students from Egypt, Malaysia, Holland, and the United States. (Courtesy of the Oracle Education Foundation.)

6. The Project Learning Institute and Success Project from St. Albans School in West Virginia. (Courtesy of the Oracle Education Foundation.)

7. Harry's Story from Kumasi, Ghana. (Courtesy of the Oracle Education Foundation.)

8. The Hydrology Project from Catalina Foothills High School in Tucson, Arizona. (Courtesy of the Pearson Foundation.)

These video case studies can also be accessed from this book's Web site—www.21stcenturyskillsbook.com—and from their respective organization Web sites:

- The Pearson Foundation: www.pearsonfoundation.org
- The Oracle Education Foundation: www.oraclefoundation.org
- The Coalition of Essential Schools: www.essentialschools.org

The complete version of the School of the Future video documentary plus other videos in the CES Essential Visions series that showcase the learning programs and principles of a variety of Coalition schools can be ordered directly from CES at www.essentialschools.org/pub/ces_docs/resources/essentialvisions.html.

Resources from the Partnership for 21st Century Skills

A rich collection of the work of the Partnership for 21st Century Skills can be found on the P21 Web site—www.21stcenturyskills .org—including detailed explanations and white papers on the skills and educational supports in the P21 framework, research studies, publications and policy reports, the results of national surveys, and a description of the work going on in a number of U.S. states to integrate 21st century skills into the fabric of everyday learning.

A special repository of resources, called "Route 21," provides a one-stop shop for 21st century skills-related information, resources, and community tools; it is available at www.21stcenturyskills.org/route21.

You are encouraged to rate the resources you use in Route 21 and to add new resources you find useful in teaching, learning, and developing 21st century skills. The goal is for Route 21 to be a universal collection of the most useful and effective resources available on 21st century learning.

Selected Online Resources

The following are online resources the authors have found informative and useful in their work on 21st century learning. This list is not intended to be exhaustive—it is merely a selection of organizations and programs the authors have found helpful in moving aspects of the 21st century skills movement forward.

Chapter Two—The Perfect Learning Storm: Four Converging Forces

A number of high-tech corporations are making substantial philanthropic investments in global programs to attract students to technical fields and to train and certify them in technical skills, building some of the essential knowledge work skills needed in the 21st century.

These so-called academy programs provide teachers, professors, and technical institute staff the training, technology tools, and curricular resources to bring their students up to certification-level competence in a variety of technical and business fields.

Three notable examples of these academy programs:

- The Cisco Networking Academy—www.cisco.com/web/learning/netacad/index.html
- The Oracle Academy—http://academy.oracle.com/
- The Microsoft IT Academy—www.microsoft.com/education/msitacademy/default.mspx

Chapter Three—Learning and Innovation Skills

One useful online guide to resources that develop critical thinking and problem solving can be found at the Foundation for Critical Thinking—www.criticalthinking.org.

There are a wealth of online resources for problem- and project-based learning that build skill in problem solving and critical thinking. Here are a few we find most helpful:

- The Illinois Math and Science Academy's Problem Based Learning Network (PBL Net)—http://pbln.imsa.edu/
- The University of Delaware's Problem Based Learning resources and clearinghouse—www.udel.edu/pbl/
- The George Lucas Educational Foundation's Edutopia resources on project learning—www.edutopia.org/ project-learning
- The Buck Foundation's project-based learning resource collection called PBL-Online—www.pbl-online.org/

Chapter Four—Digital Literacy Skills

Information Literacy Among a wealth of information literacy sources, one stands out as particularly informative and useful—the collection of online resources from the American Association of School Librarians—www.ala.org/ala/mgrps/divs/aasl/index.cfm.

These standards for 21st century learners and the accompanying resource materials clearly outline the skills needed to be an information-literate student, teacher, and librarian in our times.

Media Literacy   There are a number of helpful media literacy online resources. We've found these particularly useful:

- The Center for Media Literacy—www.medialit.org
- The Media Channel, a global community of over a thousand media education organizations—www.mediachannel.org
- The Media Clearinghouse—http://medialit.med.sc.edu
- Common Sense Media—http://commonsensemedia.org/ educators

ICT Literacy   The following organizations, most based in the United States but have an international presence, work toward the effective application of information and communication technologies in all aspects of education:

- The International Society for Technology in Education— www.iste.org/
- The Consortium for School Networking—www.cosn.org/
- The Association for Educational Communications and Technology—www.aect.org/default.asp
- Educause, an organization promoting technology integration in higher education—www.educause.edu/
- The United Nations Educational, Scientific and Cultural Organization (UNESCO) has a sector focused on ICT literacy for teachers—http://portal.unesco.org/ci/en/ev .php-URL_ID=22997&URL_DO=DO_TOPIC&URL _SECTION=201.html

One particularly strong U.S. organization that has produced a series of exemplary white papers called "Class of 2020—Action Plan for Education," which may be useful for other countries, can be found at the State Education Technology Directors Association Web site—www.setda.org/web/guest/2020.

Chapter Five—Career and Life Skills

Social and Cross-Cultural Interaction   An important resource for developing pro-social skills is the organization Educators for Social Responsibility—http://esrnational.org.

The Asia Society—http://asiasociety.org—has a wealth of resources on international and cross-cultural education.

Productivity and Accountability   In addition to the many programs and courses for new and in-service teachers at education colleges around the world, a number of corporations and foundations are also investing in the professional development of primary and secondary teachers. Many of these programs provide practicing teachers the training to integrate both technology tools and 21st century skills into their teaching methods.

Here are a few prominent examples of these teacher development programs:

- The Intel Teach program—www.intel.com/education/teach/
- Microsoft's Partners in Learning program—www.microsoft
  .com/education/pil/partnersInLearning.aspx
- Oracle Education Foundation's Professional Development programs—www.thinkquest.org/pls/html/think.help?id
  =54610
- Apple's Professional Development program—www.apple
  .com/education/leaders-administrators/professional-
  development.html

- The Pearson Foundation's Digital Arts Alliance programs—www.pearsonfoundation.org/pg4.0.html
- The Buck Institute's Project Based Learning Academies—www.bie.org/index.php/site/PBL/professional_development/#academy

Leadership and Responsibility One example of the many programs that help students develop their leadership and responsibility skills—in this case in an international context—is the Model UN program, where students simulate United Nations council meetings to resolve an international crisis—see www.nmun.org/.

Chapter Eight—Retooling Schooling

Support Systems An international organization that is pioneering large-scale assessments of some of the 21st century skills is the Organization for Economic Cooperation and Development (OECD) Programme for International Student Assessment (PISA)—www.pisa.oecd.org/pages/0,2987,en_32252351_3223 5731_1_1_1_1_1,00.html.

From Skills to Expertise: Future Learning Frameworks The vision of "whole learning for the whole child" has been well developed by the ASCD organization and its global networks and affiliates. Information about the Whole Child initiative can be found at www.ascd.org/programs/The_Whole_Child/The_Whole_Child .aspx/.

About the Partnership for 21st Century Skills

The Partnership for 21st Century Skills (P21) has pioneered a collaborative effort among educators, businesses, and governments to make 21st century learning a reality in every corner of the United States and beyond.

What Is P21?

Question: What do all of these names and organizations have in common?

- Adobe, Apple, Cisco, Dell, Ford Motor Company, HP, Intel, Lenovo, Microsoft, Oracle, Sun Microsystems, Verizon—familiar names in today's pantheon of global high-tech corporations.
- Atomic Learning, Blackboard, Cengage Learning, EF Education, Gale, K12, Lego, McGraw-Hill, Measured Progress, Pearson, Polyvision, Quarasan!, Scholastic, Thinkronize, Wireless Generation—substantial for-profit educational companies known for innovating new learning products and services.

- The American Association of School Librarians, ASCD, Cable in the Classroom, the Corporation for Public Broadcasting, Education Networks of America, Educational Testing Service, Junior Achievement, KnowledgeWorks Foundation, Learning Point Associates, the National Education Association, Sesame Street Workshop—educational nonprofit organizations providing popular learning tools, content, training, and high-impact programs for teachers, students, and schools.

Answer: All of these entities are members (as of June 2009) of an organization that has pioneered and championed the movement toward a 21st century approach to education, called the Partnership for 21st Century Skills (P21)—see http://www.21stcenturyskills.org.

Founded in 2002 as an outgrowth of a successful U.S. effort to bring the power of technology to all aspects of teaching and learning, P21 is designed to serve as "a catalyst to infuse 21st century skills throughout primary and secondary schools by building collaborative partnerships among education, business, community and government leaders." P21 has been a growing force for "preparing young people to succeed as individuals, citizens and workers in the 21st century."[1]

What Does P21 Do?

A *Time* magazine cover story in December 2006, "How to Build a Student for the 21st Century," helped launch wide public awareness of the work of P21 and its partners. The article highlighted the "yawning chasm (with an emphasis on yawning) that separates the world inside the schoolhouse from the world outside."

In 2007, P21 conducted a nationwide poll that found that nearly all voters who responded believed the teaching of 21st century skills—including critical thinking and problem solving, computer and technology skills, communication and self-direction skills—is important to the country's future economic success. This finding, and others in a long list of P21 reports, helped influence the educational agendas in the U.S. presidential election of 2008 and educational policies of the new administration.

A growing number of U.S. states have signed on to become P21 leadership states and are working to incorporate 21st century skills into all aspects of student learning, teacher professional development, curriculum, standards, assessments, and learning environments.

Although it is focused primarily on the American education system, P21's message is being echoed across the world, spreading through its network of global member organizations while like-minded advocates for educational modernization develop similar ideas in other countries. For example:

- The twenty-one-member Asia-Pacific Economic Cooperation (APEC) forum, which enlisted P21's help in formulating strategic plans for the future of education in China, Australia, Japan, Korea, Russia, Indonesia, Malaysia, Canada, and Mexico, and other countries in the region
- The United Kingdom's 21st Century Learning Alliance, which is influenced by the work and the partnering approach of P21 in its educational change agenda

- France's National Ministry of Education's *socle commun* effort to set educational goals for core knowledge and skills, which incorporates some of the P21 skills
- New Zealand's Council for Educational Research, which has a number of similarities to P21's framework in its list of "key competencies" for student learning

P21 is employing a three-part strategy to promoting and sustaining the 21st century skills agenda:

- Combining the power of three key stakeholder groups— education, business, and government—to work hand in hand toward a common vision of 21st century learning and a clear process to make it happen
- Using a broad range of communication tools—surveys, reports, magazine articles, press releases, online examples and case studies, and presentations at conferences—to get the word out about the need for 21st century skills, what they are, and how they can be learned
- Working directly with education, business, and government leaders to highlight education initiatives in their own regions (see the "Route 21" online repository of examples of 21st century learning at www.21stcenturyskills.org/route21), and to have them share their leading practices at regular summit meetings and forums

How the P21 Learning Framework Came into Being

Perhaps the most important factor of all in P21's progress has been a clear and well-articulated vision for what 21st century learning can be—the partnership's Framework for 21st Century Learning, which is used throughout this book.

A number of well-researched attempts have been carried out in the past to capture the key knowledge, skills, and learning supports needed for our times.[2] Each one was different in its categories and lists of essential skills, but none comprehensively yet simply captured the 21st century student outcomes needed plus the school reforms necessary to support those outcomes.

P21's Standards, Assessment and Professional Development Committee was assigned the job of devising a learning framework that would guide all the future work of the partnership. With more than thirty-five member organizations, a number of participating departments of education, and hundreds of members of professional education and research organizations all weighing in on what education's future should be, the committee had its hands full. Agreement seemed a very long way off.

In fact, getting to consensus on a vision for the future of learning was itself a 21st century challenge, demanding the use of all the skills the P21 committee sought to define in the framework, including collaboration, problem solving, communications, and creativity. The committee members (and the authors of this book, who co-chaired the committee) had to "eat their own cooking" as they were cooking it!

"I remember long phone conferences where we struggled to get agreement on a single compelling image that captured all the skills, knowledge, and school support systems needed for the 21st century," recalls Karen Cator, the P21 board president at the time, and the director of education leadership and advocacy at Apple, Inc. "Then suddenly, near the end of the allotted time for the meeting, someone would suggest a new phrase or combination of ideas that seemed just right, and we were off and rolling once again."

After dozens of meetings, a national conference, and endlessly updated drafts reviewed by scores of educators, business leaders, and policymakers, the framework was finally completed. The result of this collaborative effort to map the future of education in a single image (Figure B.1), and a well-articulated framing document to go with it, was well worth the year of creative consensus building it took to produce it.[3]

This P21 design has become the guidepost for the 21st century skills movement, and a road map to 21st century learning. The outcomes we expect from students today are both more rigorous and more relevant than those of the past. Applying 21st century skills, along with basic 3Rs literacy and numeracy skills, to content knowledge and 21st century themes makes for more powerful learning experiences that lead to deeper understanding and more useful knowledge in tune with our times.

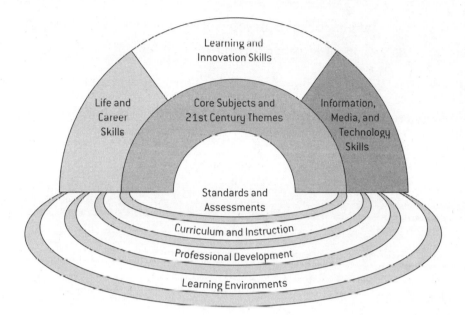

Figure B.1. **21st Century Learning Framework.**

$3Rs \times 7Cs =$ 21st Century Learning

The core subjects, themes, and skills of the P21 learning rainbow offer a memorable image of what students will need to learn to be successful in the 21st century (see Figure C.1).

To help make all of the essential 21st century skills of the P21 framework even more memorable, Table C.1 reshuffles and condenses the eleven skill sets into seven, all beginning with the letter "C."

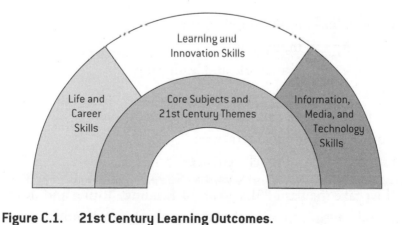

Figure C.1.   21st Century Learning Outcomes.

Table C.1.   P21 and 7C Skills.

P21 Skills	7Cs Skills
Learning and innovation skills	
Critical thinking and problem solving	Critical thinking and problem solving
Communications and collaboration	Communications, information, and media literacy
	Collaboration, teamwork, and leadership
Creativity and innovation	Creativity and innovation
Digital literacy skills	
Information literacy	[included in Communications]
Media literacy	[included in Communications]
ICT literacy	Computing and ICT literacy
Career and life skills	
Flexibility and adaptability	Career and learning self-reliance
Initiative and self-direction	[included in Career and learning self-reliance]
Social and cross-cultural interaction	Cross-cultural understanding
Productivity and accountability	[included in Career and learning self-reliance]
Leadership and responsibility	[included in Collaboration]

So we now have the "7Cs" skills of 21st century learning:

- Critical thinking and problem solving
- Creativity and innovation
- Collaboration, teamwork, and leadership
- Cross-cultural understanding
- Communications, information, and media literacy
- Computing and ICT literacy
- Career and learning self-reliance

If we take the basic "3Rs" skills of Reading, 'Riting and 'Rithmetic and multiply them by the 7Cs, we now have a handy formula for successful learning in the 21st century (and the math works too!):

$$3Rs \times 7Cs = 21st\ Century\ Learning$$

Of course, like any good formula, its value lies in its appropriate application to solving real world challenges.

As noted, the United States and the world face no more significant challenge than providing a 21st century education to every child, giving all children the chance to learn the skills to succeed as 21st century educated workers and citizens.

ACKNOWLEDGMENTS

This book is a living example of 21st century project learning at its best, with all the 21st century skills—especially collaboration, creativity, and intense communications—exercised to full capacity in its making!

We would first like to thank the entire P21 Board, and the e-Luminate Group staff, all of whom deserve major accolades for their unfailing support, and for allowing us to liberally adapt many of the core P21 materials for this book. A special mention goes to Valerie Greenhill, who has been our tireless companion and expert on the Standards, Assessments, and Professional Development Committee. Our committee has proven time and again that a wide range in viewpoints, anchored by a common goal, always makes for a better, more dynamic, and creative outcome.

We are also deeply indebted to our publisher, Jossey-Bass/ Wiley, and its incredibly supportive team: Lesley Iura, editorial director, and the extended staff and consultants: Dimi Berkner, Susan Geraghty, Sheri Gilbert, Amy Reed, and many others. You made this book a joyful experience, and your professionalism was sheer delight. It simply could not have been done without all of your seasoned contributions.

This book contains a wonderful example of collaboration between two publishing giants, as the DVD was entirely produced by the Pearson Foundation. We are deeply grateful and indebted to Mark Nieker for his open-mindedness and support, and to Stephen Brown for his tremendous professionalism.

We would also like to thank all the schools that allowed the video shooting and provided clips for use in the DVD:

- The Metropolitan Arts & Technology School, San Francisco, California
- Napa New Technology High School, Napa, California
- High Tech High, San Diego, California
- School of the Future, New York, New York
- St. Albans Elementary School, St Albans, West Virginia
- Catalina Foothills High School, Tucson, Arizona

Charles wishes to thank the following for their ideas, suggestions, guidance, inspiration, and support: Roland Acra, Vito Amato, Rupert Baines, Alex Belous, Scott Blacklin, Marli Boyle-Hagen, Pete Cevenini, John Connell, Claude Cruz, Mary Dowal, David Dusthimer, Phylis Hawkins-Miquel, Susan Jeannero, Wendy Jones, Julie Kaminkow-Sachs, Stori Lynn-Hybbeneth, Riel Miller, Lynn Osborne, Phoebe Pelobello, James Richmond, Martin Ripley, Michelle Selinger, Woody Sessoms, Christian Tawil, Tony Wagner, and Jim Wynn.

Bernie wishes to thank John Mergendoller of the Buck Institute for his help in developing the Project Learning Bicycle model, and the following for their generous support and their contributions to the thinking that went into this book: Brigid Barron, Colleen Cassity, Paul Curtis, Linda Darling-Hammond, Clare Dolan, Steven Heppell, Stuart Kahl, Jennifer Kane, Tom Kelley, Michael

Levine, Orfhlaith Ni Chorcora, Bob Pearlman, Ray Pecheone, Mitch Resnick, and Ken Robinson.

And hats off to the two authors of *Made to Stick: Why Some Ideas Survive and Others Die*, Chip and Dan Heath. Their "SUCCES" formula (simplicity, unexpectedness, concreteness, credibility, emotions, and stories) sat next to our screens during the writing of this book, guiding all our attempts to make 21st century learning as sticky as the duct tape on the cover of their book.

We'd also like to express our sincere gratitude to all our teachers and professors throughout primary, secondary, and tertiary education—particularly the least skilled ones, though well-intentioned—for providing us the eternal motivation to improve education and learning so that all children can live out their dreams and help create a better world.

| NOTES |

Chapter One

1. Stewart, 1998
2. Conference Board, Partnership for 21st Century Skills, Corporate Voices for Working Families, & Society for Human Resource Management, 2006
3. Miller, 2007
4. U.S. Bureau of Labor Statistics, 2008
5. UNESCO, 2008
6. United Nations, 1948
7. Maslow, 1987, 1998
8. Friedman, 2007

Chapter Two

1. Meieran, 2006
2. BusinessWire, 2006
3. Paschotta, 2008
4. McCain & Jukes, 2000
5. Terms noted here are from Prensky, 2001; Tapscott, 1999, 2009; and Veen, 2006. "Digital immigrants" and "do technology" are Prensky's.
6. Pew Internet Project, 2006
7. Tapscott, 2009
8. Tapscott, 2009
9. Kalantzis & Cope, 2008
10. Bransford, Brown, & Cocking, 1999; Donovan & Bransford, 2005
11. Lave & Wenger, 1991

12. Bransford, Brown, & Cocking, 1999
13. Bransford, Brown, & Cocking, 1999
14. Senge, Kleiner, Roberts, Ross, Roth, & Smith, 2000
15. Bransford, Brown, & Cocking, 1999
16. Papert, 1994
17. Goleman, 2005
18. Elias & Arnold, 2006
19. Darling-Hammond et al., 2008
20. Sternberg, 1989; Gardner, 1999; Minsky, 1988
21. Gardner, 1999
22. Tomlinson, Brimijoin, & Narvaez, 2008
23. Rose & Meyer, 2002
24. Darling-Hammond et al., 2008
25. Wenger, 1998; Wenger, McDermott, & Snyder 2002

Chapter Three

1. Levy & Murnane, 2004
2. Resnick & Hall, 1998
3. Resnick, 2007
4. Bloom & Krathwohl, 1956
5. Silva, 2008
6. Anderson & Krathwohl, 2000
7. Robinson, 2001, 2009
8. von Oech, 1989, 2008

Chapter Four

1. AASL 2007, 2009a, 2009b
2. Center for Media Literacy, n.d.
3. ISTE, 2007–2009

Chapter Five

1. Goleman, 2005, 2007

Chapter Six

1. "1.6 billion people . . . ," 2006
2. Adapted from Roger Bybee in Raizen, Sellwood, & Vickers, 1995

Chapter Seven

1. See IDEO, 2003
2. Kelley, 2002
3. Barron & Darling-Hammond, 2008
4. Darling-Hammond et al., 2008
5. Quin, Johnson, & Johnson, 1995
6. Barron, 2000, 2003
7. Darling-Hammond et al., 2008
8. Thomas, 2000
9. ELOB, 1997, 1999a, 1999b
10. Ross et al., 2001
11. Shepherd, 1998
12. Boaler, 1997, 1998
13. Penuel, Means, & Simkins, 2000
14. CTVG, 1997
15. Hmelo, Holton, & Kolodner, 2000
16. Barron et al., 1998

Chapter Eight

1. P21, 2008b
2. Becta, 2008
3. Singapore Ministry of Education, 2005
4. Marzano & Kendall, 1998
5. Darling-Hammond & Bransford, 2005
6. Law, Pellgrum, & Plomp, 2008
7. Silva, 2008
8. Silva, 2008
9. ASCD, 2007

10. "At MIT . . . ," 2009
11. Darling-Hammond & McLaughlin, 1995
12. P21, 2009b
13. Coalition for Community Schools, 2009
14. Cisco & Metiri Group, 2006
15. Fullan, 2007
16. Bransford, Brown, & Cocking, 1999

Appendix B

1. P21, 2008a
2. U.S. Department of Labor, SCANS, 1992; ISTE, 1998; AASL & AECT, 1998; Trilling & Hood, 1999; NCREL/Metiri Group, 2003
3. P21, 2008b, 2009a

| REFERENCES |

1.6 billion people around the world live without electricity. (2006, May 11). *World News*. Available online: http://archive.wn.com/ 2006/05/12/1400/p/46/4e3a55f1f01f98.html. Access date: May 10, 2009.

American Association of School Librarians. (2007). AASL standards for the 21st-century learner. Available online: http://ala.org/aasl/ standards. Access date: May 10, 2009.

American Association of School Librarians. (2009a). *Empowering learners: Guidelines for school library media programs.* Chicago: ALA.

American Association of School Librarians. (2009b). *Standards for the 21st-century learner in action.* Chicago: ALA.

Anderson, L. W., & Krathwohl, D. R. (Eds.). (2000). *A taxonomy for learning, teaching and assessing: A revision of Bloom's taxonomy of educational objectives* (complete ed.). New York: Longman.

ASCD. (2007). *The learning compact redefined: A call to action, a report of the Commission on the Whole Child.* Alexandria, VA: ASCD. (http://www.ascd.org/ASCD/pdf/Whole%20Child/WCC%20 Learning%20Compact.pdf)

At M.I.T., large lectures are going the way of blackboards. (2009, January 13). *New York Times*, p. A12.

Autor, D. (2007). Technological change and job polarization: Implications for skill demand and wage inequality. Presentation at the National Academies Workshop on Research Evidence Related to Future Skill Demands, National Academy of Science. Available online: www7.nationalacademies.org/cfe/Future_Skill_Demands _Presentations.html. Access date: May 10, 2009.

Autor, D., Levy, F., & Murnane, R. J. (2003). The skill content of recent technological change: An empirical exploration. *Quarterly Journal of Economics, 118* (November 2003), 4.

Barron, B. (2000). Problem solving in video-based microworlds: Collaborative and individual outcomes of high-achieving sixth-grade students. *Journal of the Learning Sciences, 9*(4), 403–436.

Barron, B. (2003). When smart groups fail. *Journal of the Learning Sciences, 12*(3), 307–359.

Barron, B., & Darling-Hammond, L. (2008). Powerful learning: Studies show deep understanding derives from collaborative methods. *Edutopia,* October 2008. Available online: www.edutopia.org/inquiry-project-learning-research. Access date: May 10, 2009.

Barron, B., et al. (1998). Doing with understanding: Lessons from research on problem- and project-based learning. *Journal of the Learning Sciences, 7*(3–4), 271–311.

Becta. (2008). *Harnessing technology: Next generation learning 2008–14.* Coventry, UK: Becta. Available online: http://publications.becta .org.uk/display.cfm?resID=37348. Access date: May 10, 2009.

Bloom, B. S., & Krathwohl, D. R. (1956). *Taxonomy of educational objectives, Handbook 1: Cognitive domain.* New York: Addison-Wesley.

Boaler, J. (1997). *Experiencing school mathematics, teaching styles, sex, and settings.* Buckingham, UK: Open University Press.

Boaler, J. (1998). Open and closed mathematics: Student experiences and understandings. *Journal for Research in Mathematics Education, 29,* 41–62.

Bransford, J. D., Brown, A. L., & Cocking, R. R. (Eds.). (1999). *How people learn: Brain, mind, experience and school* (expanded ed.). Washington, DC: National Academy Press.

BusinessWire. (2006, May 16). IBM researchers set world record in magnetic tape data density: 6.67 billion bits per square inch lays foundation for future tape storage improvements. *BNET,* CBS

Interactive. Available online: http://findarticles.com/p/articles/
mi_m0EIN/is_2006_May_16/ai_n26862640/?tag=content;c011.
Access date: May 10, 2009.

Center for Media Literacy. n.d. About CML. Available online: www
.medialit.org/about_cml.html. Access date: May 1, 2009.

Cisco Systems & Metiri Group. (2006). *Technology in schools:
What the research says.* San Jose, CA: Cisco Systems. Available
online: www.cisco.com/web/strategy/docs/education/
TechnologyinSchoolsReport.pdf. Access date: May 10, 2009.

Coalition for Community Schools. (2009). *Community schools research
brief 09.* Washington, DC: Author.

Cognition and Technology Group at Vanderbilt (CTGV). (1997).
*The Jasper Project: Lessons in curriculum, instruction, assessment,
and professional development.* Mahwah, NJ: Erlbaum.

Conference Board, Partnership for 21st Century Skills, Corporate
Voices for Working Families, & Society for Human Resource
Management. (2006). *Are they really ready to work? Employers'
perspectives on the basic knowledge and applied skills of new entrants
to the 21st century U.S. workforce.* New York: Conference Board.
Available online: www.21stcenturyskills.org/documents/FINAL
_REPORT_PDF09-29-06.pdf. Access date: May 10, 2009.

Darling-Hammond, L., & Bransford, J. D. (Eds.). (2005). *Preparing
teachers for a changing world: What teachers should learn and be
able to do.* San Francisco: Jossey-Bass.

Darling-Hammond, L., & McLaughlin, M. W. (1995). Policies that
support professional development in an era of reform. *Phi Delta
Kappan, 76*(8), 597–604.

Darling-Hammond, L., et al. (2008). *Powerful learning: What we know
about teaching for understanding.* San Francisco: Jossey-Bass.

Donovan, S. M., & Bransford, J. D. (Eds.). (2005). *How students learn:
History, mathematics and science in the classroom.* Washington, DC:
National Academy Press.

Elias, M. J., & Arnold, H. (2006). *The educator's guide to emotional intelligence and academic achievement: Social-emotional learning in the classroom.* Thousand Oaks, CA: Corwin Press.

Expeditionary Learning Outward Bound (ELOB). (1997). *Expeditionary Learning Outward Bound: Evidence of success.* Cambridge, MA: Author.

Expeditionary Learning Outward Bound (ELOB). (1999a). *A Design for comprehensive school reform.* Cambridge, MA: Author.

Expeditionary Learning Outward Bound (ELOB). (1999b). *Early indicators from schools implementing New American Schools designs.* Cambridge, MA: Author.

Friedman, T. L. (2007). *The world is flat 3.0: A brief history of the twenty-first century.* New York: Picador.

Friedman, T. L. (2009). *Hot, flat and crowded: Why we need a green revolution—and how it can renew America.* New York: Picador.

Fullan, M. (2007). *Leading in a culture of change* (revised ed.). San Francisco: Jossey-Bass.

Gardner, H. (1999). *Intelligence reframed: Multiple intelligences for the 21st century.* New York: Basic Books.

Goleman, D. (2005). *Emotional intelligence: Why it can matter more than IQ* (10th anniversary ed.). New York: Bantam Books.

Goleman, D. (2007). *Social intelligence: The new science of human relationships.* New York: Bantam Books.

Hmelo, C. E., Holton, D. L., & Kolodner, J. L. (2000). Designing to learn about complex systems. *Journal of the Learning Sciences, 9*(3), 247–298.

IDEO. (2003). *IDEO Method Cards: 51 ways to inspire Design.* Palo Alto, CA: IDEO.

International Society for Technology in Education (ISTE). (1998). *National Educational Technology Standards for Students (NETS-S).* Washington, DC: Author. Available online: www.iste.org/Content/ NavigationMenu/NETS/ForStudents/1998Standards/NETS_for _Students_1998_Standards.pdf. Access date: May 10, 2009.

International Society for Technology in Education (ISTE). (2007–2009). *National Educational Technology Standards for Students (NETS for Students); NETS for Teachers; NETS for Administrators.* Washington, DC: Author. Available online: www.iste.org/AM/Template.cfm?Section=NETS. Access date: May 10, 2009.

Kalantzis, M., & Cope, B. (2008). *New learning: Elements of a science of education.* Cambridge, UK: Cambridge University Press.

Kelley, T. (2002). *The art of innovation: Success through innovation the IDEO way.* London: Profile Business.

Lave, J., & Wenger, E. (1991). *Situated learning: Legitimate peripheral participation.* Cambridge, UK: Cambridge University Press.

Law, N., Pellgrum, W. J., & Plomp, T. (Eds.). (2008). *Pedagogy and ICT use in schools around the world: Findings from the IEA SITES 2006 Study.* New York: Springer.

Levy, F., & Murnane, R. J. (2004). *The new division of labor: How computers are creating the next job market.* Princeton, NJ: Princeton University Press.

Marzano, R. J., & Kendall, J. S. (1998). *Awash in a sea of standards.* Denver, CO: McREL. Available online: www.mcrel.org/PDF/Standards/5982IR_AwashInASea.pdf. Access date: May 10, 2009.

Maslow, A. H. (1987). *Motivation and personality* (3rd ed.). New York: HarperCollins.

Maslow, A. H. (1998). *Toward a psychology of being* (3rd ed.). New York: Wiley.

McCain, T., & Jukes, I. (2000). *Windows on the future: Education in the age of technology.* Thousand Oaks, CA: Corwin Press.

Meieran, E. (2006, September). Back to the future, part IV: Moore's Law, the legend, and the man. *IEEE Solid State Circuits Journal.*

Miller, R. (2007). *Education and economic growth: From the 19th to the 21st century.* San Jose, CA: Cisco Systems. Available online: www.rielmiller.com/images/Education-and-Economic-Growth.pdf. Access date: May 10, 2009.

Minsky, M. (1988). *The society of mind.* New York: Simon & Schuster.

National Center on Education and the Economy. (2007). *Tough choices or tough times: The report of the new commission on the skills of the American workforce.* San Francisco: Jossey-Bass.

North Central Regional Educational Laboratory (NCREL) & the Metiri Group. (2003). *EnGauge: 21st century skills.* Naperville, IL: NCREL. Available online: http://www.unctv.org/education/teachers_childcare/nco/documents/skillsbrochure.pdf. Access date: May 10, 2009.

Papert, S. A. (1994). *The children's machine: Rethinking school in the age of the computer.* New York: Basic Books.

Partnership for 21st Century Skills (P21). (2007). *Beyond the three Rs: Voter attitudes toward 21st century skills.* Tucson, AZ: Author. Available online: www.21stcenturyskills.org/documents/P21 _pollreport_singlepg.pdf. Access date: May 10, 2009.

Partnership for 21st Century Skills (P21). (2008a). *Moving education forward.* Tucson, AZ: Author. Available online: www .21stcenturyskills.org/documents/p21_brochure_-final4.pdf. Access date: May 10, 2009.

Partnership for 21st Century Skills (P21). (2008b). *21st century skills in West Virginia.* Tucson, AZ: Author. Available online: www.21stcenturyskills.org/documents/p21_wv2008.pdf. Access date: May 10, 2009.

Partnership for 21st Century Skills (P21). (2009a). *Framework for 21st century learning.* Tucson, AZ: Author. Available online: www.21stcenturyskills.org/documents/framework_flyer_updated _jan_09_final-1.pdf. Access date: May 10, 2009.

Partnership for 21st Century Skills (P21). (2009b). *21st century learning environments* (white paper). Tucson, AZ: Author. Available online: www.21stcenturyskills.org/documents/le_white_paper-1 .pdf. Access date: May 10, 2009.

Paschotta, R. (2008). *Encyclopedia of laser physics and technology.* Berlin: Wiley-VCH. Available online: www.rp-photonics.com/ optical_fiber_communications.html. Access date: May 10, 2009.

Penuel, W. R., Means, B., & Simkins, M. B. (2000). The multimedia challenge. *Educational Leadership, 58,* 34–38.

Pew Internet Project. (2006). Digital natives: How today's youth are different from their "digital immigrant" elders and what that means for libraries. Presentation at Metro—New York City Library Council, October 27, 2006. Available online: www.pewinternet.org/~/media//Files/Presentations/2006/2006%20-%2010.27.06%20Metro%20NY%20Library%20-%20final%20.ppt.ppt). Access date: May 10, 2009.

Prensky, M. (2001, October). Digital natives, digital immigrants. *On the Horizon, 9*(5).

Quin, Z., Johnson, D., & Johnson, R. (1995). Cooperative versus competitive efforts and problem solving. *Review of Educational Research, 65*(2), 129–143.

Raizen, S. B., Sellwood, P., & Vickers, M. (1995). *Technology education in the classroom: Understanding the designed world.* San Francisco: Jossey-Bass.

Resnick, L. B. (2007). Principles of learning. Institute for Learning. Web site. Available online: http://ifl.lrdc.pitt.edu/ifl/index.php?section=pol. Access date: May 10, 2009.

Resnick, L. B., & Hall, M. W. (1998). Learning organizations for sustainable education reform. *Daedalus, 127*(4), 89–118.

Resnick, L. B., & Resnick, D. P. (1992). Assessing the thinking curriculum: New tools for educational reform. In *Changing assessments: Alternative views of aptitude, achievement, and instruction.* B. R. Gifford & M. C. O'Connor, (Eds.). Boston: Kluwer Academic.

Robinson, K. (2001). *Out of our minds: Learning to be creative.* Chichester, UK: Capstone.

Robinson, K. (2009). *The element: How finding your passion changes everything.* New York: Viking Press.

Rose, D. H., & Meyer, A. (2002). *Teaching every student in the digital age: Universal design for learning.* Alexandria, VA: ASCD.

Ross, S. M., et al. (2001). Two- and three-year achievement results on the Tennessee Value-Added Assessment System for Restructuring Schools in Memphis. *School Effectiveness and School Improvement, 12,* 323–346.

Senge, P., Kleiner, A., Roberts, C., Ross, R., Roth, G., & Smith, B. (2000). *Schools that learn: A fifth discipline fieldbook for educators, parents, and everyone who cares about education.* New York: Doubleday.

Shepherd, H. G. (1998). The probe method: A problem-based learning model's effect on critical thinking skills of fourth- and fifth-grade social studies students. *Dissertation Abstracts International, Section A: Humanities and Social Sciences, 59*(3-A).

Silva, E. (2008). *Measuring skills for the 21st century.* Washington, DC: Education Sector.

Singapore Ministry of Education. (2005). *Teach less, learn more: To engage our learners and prepare them for life.* Singapore: Ministry of Education. Available online: www3.moe.edu.sg/bluesky/images/ TLLM_Journal2.pdf. Access date: May 10, 2009.

Sternberg, R. J. (1989). *The triarchic mind: A new theory of human intelligence.* New York: Penguin.

Stewart, T. A. (1998). *Intellectual capital: The new wealth of organizations.* New York: Currency/Doubleday.

Tapscott, D. (1999). *Growing up digital: The rise of the net generation.* New York: McGraw-Hill.

Tapscott, D. (2009). *Grown up digital: How the net generation is changing your world.* New York: McGraw-Hill.

Thomas, J. W. (2000). *A review of research on project based learning.* Paper prepared for The Autodesk Foundation, San Rafael, CA. Available online: www.bie.org/files/researchreviewPBL_1.pdf. Access date: May 10, 2009.

Tomlinson, C. A., Brimijoin, K., & Narvaez, L. (2008). *The differentiated school: Making revolutionary changes in teaching and learning.* Alexandria, VA: ASCD.

Trilling, B., & Hood, P. (1999). Learning, technology, and education reform in the knowledge age, or "we're wired, webbed and windowed, now what?" *Educational Technology Magazine,* May/June 1999. Englewood Cliffs, NJ: Educational Technology Publications. Available online: www.wested.org/online_pubs/learning_technology.pdf. Access date: May 10, 2009.

UNESCO. (2008). *Education for All global monitoring report 2009.* Oxford: Oxford University Press.

United Nations. (1948). *The universal declaration of human rights, article 26.* New York: United Nations. Available online: www.un.org/Overview/rights.html#a26. Access date: May 10, 2009.

U.S. Bureau of Labor Statistics. (2008). *Number of jobs held, labor market activity, and earnings growth among the youngest baby boomers: Results from a longitudinal survey.* Washington, DC: U.S. Department of Labor. Available online: www.bls.gov/news.release/pdf/nlsoy.pdf. Access date: May 10, 2009.

U.S. Department of Labor, Secretary's Commission on Achieving Necessary Skills (SCANS). (1992). *Learning a living: A blueprint for high performance.* Washington, DC: U.S. Department of Labor.

Veen, W. (2006). *Homo zappiens: Growing up in a digital age.* London: Network Continuum Education.

Von Oech, R. (1989). *Creative Whack Pack.* Stamford, CT: US Games Systems.

Von Oech, R. (2009). *A whack on the side of the head: How you can be more creative* (25th anniversary ed.). New York: Business Plus.

Wenger, E. (1999). *Communities of practice: Learning, meaning, and identity.* Cambridge, UK: Cambridge University Press.

Wenger, E., McDermott, R., & Snyder, W. M. (2002). *Cultivating communities of practice: A guide to managing knowledge.* Boston, MA: Harvard Business Press.

CREDITS

Figure 1.3. New Skills for 21st Century Work:

- Adapted from *The New Division of Labor: How Computers Are Creating the Next Job Market* by Frank Levy and Richard J. Murnane. Copyright © 2004 by Russell Sage Foundation. Published by Princeton University Press.

Figure 3.1. SARS screenshot:

- All rights reserved. Reprinted by permission of the Oracle Education Foundation.

Figure 3.3. *Creative Whack Pack Creativity Cards:*

- From *Roger von Oech's Creative Whack Pack®*. Copyright © 1992 Roger von Oech. All rights reserved. Reprinted by permission of Roger von Oech, http://tinyurl.com/whackpack.

Figure 6.1. Science and Technology, Questions and Problems:

- Adapted from Roger Bybee in *Technology Education in the Classroom: Understanding the Designed World* by Senta A. Raizen, Peter Sellwood, Ronald D. Todd, and Margaret Vickers. Copyright © 1995 by Jossey-Bass Inc., Publishers.

Figure 7.1. Student and Teacher Project Wheels:

- Adapted with permission from the Oracle Education Foundation.

Figures 7.2 and 7.3. Project Learning Bicycle figures:

- Adapted with permission from the Oracle Education Foundation.

Figure 8.1. Systems Diagram of School Interactions:

- From *Schools That Learn: A Fifth Discipline Fieldbook for Teachers, Administrators, Parents, and Everyone Who Cares About Education* by Peter Senge, Art Kleiner, Charlotte Roberts, Rick Ross, George Roth, and Bryan Smith. Copyright © 2000 by Peter Senge, Art Kleiner, Charlotte Roberts, Rick Ross, George Roth, and Bryan Smith. Reprinted by permissions of Doubleday, a division of Random House, Inc., and The Spieler Agency.

Figure 8.2. 21st Century Learning Framework:

- Copyright © Partnership for 21st Century Skills. Reprinted by permission of the Partnership for 21st Century Skills, www.21stcenturyskills.org.

Figure 8.4. 21st Century Classroom Design:

- From *Designing Spaces for Effective Learning: A Guide to 21st Century Learning Space Design* published by JISC, 2006. Reprinted by permission of AMA Alexi Marmot Associates and JISC.

HOW TO USE THE DVD

* If you are reading this material in an electronic book format and need access to the content on the DVD, please visit the book's Web site, where you will find directions for viewing the video clips:

www.21stcenturyskillsbook.com

System Requirements

PC with Microsoft Windows 98 or later
Mac with Apple OS version 10 or later
TV with DVD player
You will also need:
Quicktime 7.0 or later (available at www.apple.com)
Adobe Acrobat Reader 8.0 or later (available at www.adobe.com)

Using the DVD

1. Insert the DVD into your computer's DVD drive or your TV DVD player.
2. If you are using a PC, the DVD should automatically begin to run and give you the options for viewing the videos. You MUST have Quicktime to view the videos, and you MUST have Adobe Acrobat Reader to use the PDFs. If the DVD does not immediately begin to run, go to "My Computer" and double click on your computer's DVD drive. The DVD should begin to run.

3. If you are working on a Mac, click the DVD icon that appears on your desktop. Then click the "JB" icon that appears in the window that opens. The DVD should begin to run and give you the options for viewing the videos.

In Case of Trouble

If you experience difficulty using the DVD, please follow these steps:

1. Make sure your hardware and systems configurations conform to the systems requirements noted under "System Requirements" above.
2. Review the installation procedure for your type of hardware and operating system.

To speak with someone in Product Technical Support, call 800-762-2974 or 317-572-3994 M–F 8:30 A.M.–5:00 P.M. EST. You can also get support and contact Product Technical Support through our Web site at www.wiley.com/techsupport.

Before calling or writing, please have the following information available:

• Type of computer and operating system
• Any error messages displayed
• Complete description of the problem.

It is best if you are sitting at your computer when making the call.

INDEX

A

Accountability, skills for, 82–83, 165–166
Adaptability, skills for, 75–77
Agrarian Age, 13, 14–15
American Association of School Librarians (AASL), 66
Assessments: progress being made in, 130–134; as support system in P21 learning framework, 119
Authentic learning, 31
Automobile industry, 21, 22, 23

B

Bacterial Transformation Lab: described, 96; Project Learning Bicycle model followed by, 97–98, 101, 102–103; video of, 95
Boyer, E., 61
Brown, D. B., 137

C

Career skills. See Life and career skills
Cator, K., 171–172
Center for Media Literacy, 68
Change: exercise on, and future of education, xxx–xxxiv; in role of education, xxix. See also Forces of change
Chien, A., 95, 96, 97–98
Children, number enrolled in schools, 11
Chinese Ministry of Education, visit to American school by, xxv–xxvii
Cognition and Technology Group at Vanderbilt University (CTGV), 112
Collaboration skills, 54–56
Collaborative inquiry, obstacles to, 114–115

Collaborative small-group learning, 108–109
College Work and Readiness Assessment (CWRA), 132
Communication skills, 54–56
Content: current research on mastery of, 50–51; progress in standards on, 125–130; teaching skills vs., 36, 38, 39
Coordination of support systems, 122
Creative Whack Pack Creativity Cards, 58, 60
Creativity: Chinese desire for curriculum to teach, xxv–xxvii; education as stifling, 57; skills for, 56–60; through learning projects, 104–107
Critical thinking skills, 50–54
Cross-cultural interaction, skills for, 80–81, 165
Curriculum: progress being made in, 134–136; as support system in P21 learning framework, 119; to teach creativity and innovation, xxv–xxvii

D

Darling-Hammond, L., 108
Design process, IDEO, 105–107
Design-based learning (design): defined, 94; examples of, 112–113; obstacles to, 114–115. See also Engineering design method
Developed countries, creative work in, 9, 10
Developing countries, routine work in, 9, 10
Diamond, J., xxxix

Digital devices: digital lifestyle based on, 27–30; as thinking tools, 25

Digital lifestyles, as force shaping 21st century learning, 21, 23, 27–30

Digital literacy skills, 61–71; and 7C skills, 176; fable about, 61–64; for ICT literacy, 68–70, 71, 164–165; for information literacy, 65–67, 163; for media literacy, 67–68, 69, 164; online resources on, 163–165

Digital natives. *See* Net geners

Diversity, skills to deal with, 80–81

Drucker, P., 82, 151

DVD: how to use, 199–200; video case studies on, 159–160

E

Edison, T., 91

Education: changed role of, xxix; creativity stifled by, 57; declared fundamental right of children, 11; examples of 21st century, throughout globe, 154–155; exercise on future of, xxx–xxxiv; forces resisting change in, 35–36; impact on income, 8, 9; importance of, in 21st century, 40–41, 152–153, 156–157; as prerequisite for knowledge work, 6; role in 21st century, 15–19; role in quality of life, 156–157; work skills not taught by, 7. *See also* Schools; 21st century education system initiatives

Educational goals: in Agrarian Age, 13, 14–15; in Industrial Age, 13–15; in Knowledge Age, 14–19; universal, 12–13

Educators for Social Responsibility (ESR), 80

Einstein, A., 90, 104

Engineering design method: problems as basis of, 91; scientific experimental method vs., 92, 93. *See also* Design-based learning (design)

Expertise: education for developing, 6, 10; on expertise, 146–147; as link in Knowledge Age value chain, 4, 146

F

FIRST Robotics contests, 105, 113

Flexibility: skills for, 75–77; in use of time, 141

Forbes, S., 151

Forces of change: resisting new model of 21st century learning, 35–36; shaping 21st century learning model, 21, 23, 24–34; shaping automobile industry jobs, 21, 22, 23

Formative assessments, 130–131, 134

Four Questions exercise, xxx–xxxiv, 122

Friedman, T. L., 5

Fuller, B., 151

Funding, for 21st century education system initiatives, 123

G

Gandhi, I., 89

H

Hall, M., 50

Hoffer, E., 75

I

ICT literacy, 68–70, 71, 164–-165

IDEO, design process of, 105–107

Income, education's impact on, 8, 9

Industrial Age: educational goals in, 13–15; shift from, to Knowledge Age, 3–5; value chain for, 4

Information literacy, 65–67, 163

Initiative, skills for, 77–79

Innovation: Chinese desire for curriculum to teach, xxv–xxvii; skills for, 56–60. *See also* Learning and innovation skills

Innovation Age: Knowledge Age being replaced by, 56–57; project learning to prepare for, 104, 105, 107

Inquiry-based learning (inquiry): defined, 94; obstacles to, 114–115. *See also* Scientific experimental method

Instructional methods: progress being made in, 134–136; shifting, toward 21st century learning model, 36–40; as support system in P21 learning framework, 119; tools to support, 89–90

Intel Teach program, 136, 165

Intelligences, multiple, 33–34

International Society for Technology in Education (ISTE), 70

J

Jobs: automobile industry, 21, 22, 23; lifetime total of, 10; skills required for 21st century, 8–9, 11, 24–25. *See also* Work

K

Kay, A., 146

Kelley, T., 105

Kennedy, J. F., 89

Knowledge Age: educational goals in, 14–19; Innovation Age replacing, 56–57; shift from Industrial Age to, 3–5; value chain for, 4, 146

Knowledge work: education as prerequisite for, 6; as force shaping 21st century learning, 21, 23, 24–25; increase in, 5; skills required for, 8–9, 24–25

Knowledge-and-Skills Rainbow, 47–48

L

Leadership: as principle for 21st century education system initiatives, 123–124; progress being made in, 143, 145; skills for, 84–85, 166

Learning: authentic, 31; changed role of, xxix; current global environment for, 153–154; exercise on future of, xxx–xxxiv; fable about Internet's influence on, 61–64; formula for, in 21st century, 175–177; social, 34; taxonomy for, 50–51; tools to support, 89–90; whole, 148–149, 166

Learning and innovation skills, 48, 49–60; and 7C skills, 176; communication and collaboration as, 54–56; creativity and innovation as, 56–60; critical thinking and problem solving as, 50–54; importance of, 49–50; online resources for, 163

Learning communities, 143, 144, 148, 149

Learning environments: progress being made in, 139–145; as support system in P21 learning framework, 119

Learning framework. *See* P21 learning framework

Learning methods: based on problems, 94, 111–115; based on questions, 94, 114–115; collaborative small-group, 108–109; research on effectiveness of, 107–113; shifting, toward 21st century learning model, 36–40; tools to support, 89–90. *See also* Learning projects

Learning model. *See* 21st century learning model

Learning projects: characteristics of effective, 109; compared to other learning methods, 109–111; creativity through, 104–107; obstacles to, 114–115; productivity and accountability skills developed by, 82; Project Learning Bicycle as model for, 96–102; research on effectiveness of, 107–114; resources on, 135–136, 159–161; teacher's reflections on, 95. *See also* Bacterial Transformation Lab; SARS Project

Learning research, as force shaping 21st century learning, 21, 23, 30–34

Learning societies, 148, 149

Librarians, 66

Life and career skills, 73–86; and 7C skills, 176; for flexibility and adaptability, 75–77; for initiative and self-direction, 77–79; for leadership and responsibility, 84–85; online resources on, 165–166;

Life and career skills, *continued*
as performance evaluation criteria,
73–74; for productivity and accountability, 82–83; for social and cross-
cultural interaction, 80–81

Ling, T. L., 37

Literacy rate, economic impact of, 8

M

Maslow, A., 12

Massachusetts Institute of Technology
(MIT), introductory physics class
format, 135

Media literacy, 67–68, 69, 164

Mental model building, 32

Models: mental, 32; Project Learning
Bicycle, 96–102; studio, of work,
84–85. *See also* 21st century learning
model

Motivation: internal, 33; problems as,
90–91, 93–94; questions as, 90,
93–94

Multiple intelligences, 33–34

N

Napa New Tech High School, Chinese
officials' visit to, xxv–xxvii

Net geners: digital lifestyle of, 27–30;
global learning network being created
by, 153; technology used for learning
by, 69, 142

New Tech Foundation, 37

O

Obama, B., xxxix, 18, 84

Online resources: academy programs,
162; on digital literacy skills, 163–165;
on learning and innovation skills,
163; on life and career skills, 165–166;
Partnership for 21st Century Skills
(P21), 161, 168; "Route 21," 161, 170;
video case studies, 160–161

Oracle Education Foundation: Project
Learning Institute, 82, 136, 160;
teacher development program, 165;
Web site, 46, 160

P

P21 learning framework: diagram of, 119;
history of development of, 170–172;
Knowledge-and-Skills Rainbow of,
47–48; support systems in, 117, 119.
See also Partnership for 21st Century
Skills (P21)

Paine, S., 117, 120

Partnership for 21st Century Skills (P21),
167–173; consensus-building activity
from, xxx–xxxiv, 122; described, 45;
digital literacy skills described by, 67,
69, 71; learning and innovation skills
described by, 52, 55, 59; life and career
skills described by, 77, 79, 81, 83, 85;
members of, 167–168; purpose of,
168; resources from, 161; Web site,
161, 168; work of, 168–170. *See also*
P21 learning framework

Pearlman, B., 37

Performance evaluation, life and career
skills as criteria in, 73–74

Policy, official, as principle for 21st
century education system initiatives,
122–123

*Powerful Learning: What We Know About
Teaching for Understanding* (Darling-
Hammond et al.), 108

Problem solving skills, 50–54

Problem-based learning, 111–112

Problems: as basis of engineering design
method, 91; humans' power to solve,
89; learning methods based on, 94,
111–115; as motivators, 90–91, 93–94.
See also Learning projects

Productivity, skills for, 82–83, 165–166

Professional development, teacher: examples of programs for, 165–166; as
principle for 21st century education
system initiatives, 124–125; progress
being made in, 136–139; as support
system in P21 learning framework, 119

Project learning. *See* Learning projects
Project Learning Bicycle model: Bacterial Transformation Lab as following, 102–103; overview of, 96–102
Projects. *See* Learning projects

Q

Quality of life, education's role in, 156–157
Questions: as basis of scientific experimental method, 90, 91; learning method based on, 94, 114–115; as motivators, 90, 93–94; power of, 89, 90

R

Resnick, D., 130
Resnick, L., 50, 130
Responsibility, skills for, 84–85, 166
Reynolds, P., 104
Riley, R., 3
Robinson, K., 57
"Route 21" resources, 161, 170

S

SARS Project: communication and collaboration skills used in, 54, 56; creativity and innovation skills used in, 58; critical thinking and problem solving skills used in, 51, 53; described, 46–47; as example of design-based learning, 112; flexibility and adaptability skills used in, 76; information literacy skills used in, 65–66; initiative and self-direction skills used in, 78; leadership and responsibility skills used in, 84; social and cross-cultural skills used in, 81
School of the Future (New York City), 96
Schools: changes in, to support 21st century learning, 139–141; number of children enrolled in, 11; U.S. vs. Chinese, xx. *See also* Education
Scientific experimental method: engineering design method vs., 92, 93; questions as basis of, 90, 91. *See also* Inquiry-based learning (inquiry)

Self-direction, skills for, 77–79
Singapore, "Teach Less, Learn More" initiative, 36–37, 121, 128
Skills: and 21st Century Knowledge-and-Skills Rainbow, 47–48; lacking in graduates of education facilities, 7; required for 21st century jobs, 8–9, 11, 24–25; STEAM, 104; STEM, 24, 104. *See also* 21st century skills
Slavin, R., 114
Social interaction, skills for, 80–81, 165
Social learning, 34
Standards: progress being made in, 125–130; as support system in P21 learning framework, 119
STEAM skills, 104
STEM skills/subjects, 24, 104
Studio model, 84–85
Summative assessments, 130, 131–132, 133
Support systems, 125–145; assessments as, 130–134; coordination of, 122; curriculum and instruction as, 134–136; learning environments as, 139–145; online resources on, 166; P21 approach to, 117, 119; standards as, 125–130; systems diagram of, 118; teacher professional development as, 136–139

T

Taxonomy for learning, 50–51
Teachers, professional development of, 119, 124–125, 136–139, 165–166
Teaching methods. *See* Instructional methods
Technology: assessments based on, 132, 133, 134; digital lifestyle based on, 27–30; examples of schools throughout world utilizing, 154–156; to personalize learning, 34; as principle for 21st century education system initiatives, 124; progress being made in, to aid learning, 142; supporting shift to 21st century learning model, 40; as thinking tool, 25. *See also* ICT literacy

Testing. *See* Assessments

Thinking tools, as force shaping 21st century learning, 21, 23, 25–27

ThinkQuest Web site competition, 46, 105. *See also* SARS Project

Toffler, A., xxxix

21st century: challenges of, 5–6; formula for learning in, 175–177; importance of education in, 40–41, 152–153, 156–157; role of education in, 15–19

21st century education system initiatives: principles shared by, 121–125; tools needed to support, 89–90. *See also* West Virginia's 21st Century Learning initiative

21st century learning framework. *See* P21 learning framework

21st century learning model: forces converging to shape, 21, 23, 24–34; forces resisting shift to, 35–36; future of, 148–150, 166; Project Learning Bicycle as, 96–102; shifting teaching and learning practices toward, 36–40

21st century skills: digital literacy skills as, 48, 61–71, 163–165, 176; examples of schools throughout world teaching, 154–156; learning and innovation skills as, 48, 49–60, 163, 176; life and career skills as, 48, 73–86, 165–166, 176; SARS Project as example of developing, 46–47; 7 Cs of, 175–177; used in Bacterial Transformation Lab, 103; video case studies of, 159–161

U

United Kingdom, "Harnessing Technology: Next Generation Learning 2008–14," 121

United Nations: declared education fundamental right of children, 11; Model UN program, 85, 166; UNESCO's efforts for ICT literacy, 70, 164

Universal Design for Learning, 34

V

Value chains, Knowledge vs. Industrial Age, 4, 146

Vision, as principle for 21st century education system initiatives, 121–122

von Oech, R., 58, 60

W

Web sites: competitions to create, 105. *See also* Online resources

West Virginia's 21st Century Learning initiative: assessments in, 132, 133; goals of, 120; redesigned standards of, 126, 127, 128–129; teacher professional development effort of, 136–138

Whole learning, 148–149, 166

Work: routine vs. creative, 9, 10; studio model of, 84–85. *See also* Jobs; Knowledge work

Work skills. *See* Life and career skills